MW00817786

Wisdom of Solomon

T&T Clark Study Guides

Series Editors
Michael A. Knibb, A. T. Lincoln
and R. N. Whybray

Titles in the T&T Clark Study Guides series

Wisdom of Solomon

Lester L. Grabbe

T&T Clark Study Guides

Series Editors
Michael A. Knibb, A. T. Lincoln
and R. N. Whybray

T&T CLARK INTERNATIONAL
A Continuum imprint
LONDON • NEW YORK

T&T Clark International, a Continuum imprint

The Tower Building, 11 York Road, London SE1 7NX
15 East 26th Street, Suite 1703, New York, NY 10010

www.tandtclark.com

Copyright © 1997 Sheffield Academic Press

First published by Sheffield Academic Press in 1997
Reprinted by T&T Clark International in 2003

British Library Cataloguing-in-Publication Data
A catalogue record for this book is available from the British Library

ISBN 0-567-08444-2

Typeset by Sheffield Academic Press
Printed on acid-free paper in Great Britain by Cromwell Press, Wiltshire

Contents

Preface

This book has a very simple purpose. As the series in which it appears is entitled, it is a *guide* to the student in studying the Wisdom of Solomon. Many readers may come to it with the hope of being told various things about the book: authorship, date of writing, audience, and the like. They may expect it to give them definitive information on such subjects. These subjects are indeed discussed here, but the aim of this volume is not to be a definitive work of reference. On the contrary, it is meant to be suggestive and illustrative. It will show how some scholars have answered the questions or approached them, but it will not necessarily tell you *the* answer on any particular topic. My ultimate aim is to give the student the tools to investigate for oneself.

Translations of Wisdom of Solomon are from the New Revised Standard Version unless otherwise indicated. Quotations from classical Greek and Latin literature are taken from the Loeb Classical Library (London: Heinemann; Cambridge, MA: Harvard), as are those from Josephus and Philo.

This book is dedicated to two former professors of the Hull Theology Department: Professor Emeritus R.N. Whybray and the late Revd Professor A.T. Hanson. These two men took retirement in 1982, and I joined the department in that year. I was *de facto* the replacement for Norman, but for complicated reasons I was really *de jure* the replacement for Anthony. Norman Whybray is an internationally recognized specialist in the wisdom literature of the Hebrew Bible and Early Judaism, but Anthony Hanson included both Old and New Testament wisdom in his interests.

Text, Commentaries, and Other Studies

Texts

Emerton, John A., and David J. Lane (eds.), *Wisdom of Solomon* (Old Testament in Syriac, 2.5; Leiden: Brill, 1979). A critical edition of the Peshitta version.

Stein, Edmund, *'Sefer Ḥokmat Šĕlōmō', ha-Sĕfōrîm ha-Ḥîṣônîm* (ed. Abraham Kehana; Tel-Aviv, 1936; repr. Jerusalem: Makor, 1978) II, 363–414. A translation of the Wisdom of Solomon into vocalized Hebrew, with introduction and notes.

Thiele, W. (ed.), *Sapientia Salomonis* (Vetus Latina; Freiberg: Herder, 1977–86). A critical text of the Old Latin version.

Ziegler, J., *Sapientia Salomonis* (Septuaginta, Vetus Testamentum Graecum, 12.1; Göttingen: Vandenhoeck & Ruprecht, 2nd edn, 1980). The main critical text. It contains all the linguistic information even if one differs from the editor about the reconstructed text.

Commentaries

Clarke, E.G., *The Wisdom of Solomon* (Cambridge Bible Commentary on the New English Bible; Cambridge: Cambridge: University Press, 1973). Designed for the lay person and non-specialist.

Georgi, Dieter, *Weisheit Salomos* (Jüdische Schriften aus hellenistisch–römischer Zeit, III.4; Gütersloh: Mohn, 1980): 391–478. Part of a well-known series of Hellenistic Jewish literature in German translation with introduction and brief notes.

Grimm, C.L.W., *Das Buch der Weisheit erklärt* (Kurzgefasstes exegetisches Handbuch zu den Apokryphen, 6; Leipzig: Hirzel, 1860). A classic commentary which still has value.

Holmes, Samuel, 'The Wisdom of Solomon', *The Apocrypha and Pseudepigrapha of the Old Testament in English* (ed. R.H. Charles; Oxford: Clarendon, 1913): II, 518–68. Part of a classic set which still has much value.

Larcher, C., OP, *Le Livre de la Sagesse ou la Sagesse de Salomon* (3 vols.; Etudes Bibliques, nouvelle série, 1; Paris: Gabalda, 1983–85). A French *magnum opus* covering all aspects of scholarship on the book, including a 161-page introduction.

Reider, J., *The Book of Wisdom* (Jewish Apocryphal Literature; New York: Dropsie College, 1957). A text, translation, and brief commentary aimed at the student and scholar.

Winston, David, *The Wisdom of Solomon: A New Translation with Introduction and Commentary* (AB, 43; Garden City, NY: Doubleday, 1979). The standard commentary in English.

Other Studies

Collins, John J., *Between Athens and Jerusalem: Jewish Identity in the Hellenistic Diaspora* (New York: Crossroad, 1986). An incisive survey of much of the early Jewish literature in Greek, with the exception of Philo and Josephus.

Dalbert, Peter, *Die Theologie der hellenistisch-jüdischen Missionsliteratur unter Ausschluss von Philo und Josephus* (Theologische Forschung, 4; Hamburg–Volksdorf: Herbert Reich, 1954). The teachings of some of the main early Jewish writings, especially those which might be aimed at outsiders. See pp. 70-92 on the Wisdom of Solomon.

Focke, Friedrich, *Die Entstehung der Weisheit Salomos: Ein Beitrag zur Geschichte des jüdischen Hellenismus* (FRLANT, 22; Göttingen: Vandenhoeck & Ruprecht, 1913). An important early study attempting to determine the origin of the book.

Gilbert, M., SJ, *La critique des dieux dans le Livre de la Sagesse (Sg 13–15)* (AB, 53; Rome: Biblical Institute, 1973). A detailed exegesis of the passage attacking idol worship (Wis. 13–15).

—'Wisdom of Solomon', in *Jewish Writings of the Second Temple Period: Apocrypha, Pseudepigrapha, Qumran Sectarian Writings, Philo, Josephus* (ed. M.E. Stone; Compendia Rerum Iudaicarum ad Novum Testamentum, 2.2; Assen: Van Gorcum; Minneapolis: Fortress Press, 1984): 301-13. An introduction to the Wisdom of Solomon in English, part of a major survey of Jewish literature of the Second Temple period.

—'Sagesse de Salomon (ou Livre de la Sagesse)', in *Supplément au Dictionnaire de la Bible* (ed. J. Briend and E. Cothenet; Paris: Letouzey & Ané, 1986): XI, 58-119. A standard recent introduction, more detailed than the previous work in English.

Grabbe, Lester L., *Judaism from Cyrus to Hadrian* (Minneapolis: Fortress Press, 1992; London: SCM Press, 1994). A history of Second Temple Judaism, mainly concerned with Palestine but also containing references to Jewish communities in Egypt and elsewhere. Includes an extensive guide to recent scholarship and bibliography.

—*An Introduction to First-Century Judaism: Religion and Politics 539 BCE to 135 CE* (Edinburgh: T. & T. Clark, 1996). An entrée into the subject aimed at the general reader, covering some of the same ground as the previous work but less detailed.

Kolarcik, Michael, *The Ambiguity of Death in the Book of Wisdom 1–6: A Study of Literary Structure and Interpretation* (AnBib, 127; Rome: Pontifical Biblical Institute, 1991). The main concern is with the question of the Wisdom of Solomon's view about immortality, but there is much discussion of literary structure.

Larcher, C., OP, *Etudes sur le Livre de la Sagesse* (EBib; Paris: Gabalda, 1969). A collection of studies on different aspects of the Wisdom of Solomon by a noted expert.

Nickelsburg, G.W.E., *Resurrection, Immortality, and Eternal Life in Intertestamental Judaism* (Harvard Theological Studies, 26; Cambridge, MA: Harvard, 1972). Still the main study on the subject, including the Wisdom of Solomon.

—*Jewish Literature between the Bible and the Mishnah* (Philadelphia: Fortress Press, 1981). An important introduction to and survey of Jewish literature of the Second Temple period.

Pfeiffer, Robert H., *History of New Testament Times, with an Introduction to the Apocrypha* (New York: Harper, 1949). A summary of scholarship on the Apocrypha up to the time of writing.

Reese, James M., *Hellenistic Influence on the Book of Wisdom and its Consequences* (AnBib, 41; Rome: Pontifical Biblical Institute, 1970). An important study on various aspects of the book, especially in relation to Greek literature and rhetoric.

Schürer, E., 'The Wisdom of Solomon', in *The History of the Jewish People in the Age of Jesus Christ (175 BC–AD 135)* (ed. G. Vermes, F. Millar and M. Goodman; Edinburgh: T. & T. Clark, 1973–86): III, 568-79. Schürer's three-volume work is a major reference work on Judaism in the Greek and early Roman period. The last volume (in two parts) surveys the literature.

Schwenk-Bressler, Udo, *Sapientia Salomonis als ein Beispiel frühjüdischer Textauslegung: Die Auslegung des Buches Genesis, Exodus 1–15 und Teilen der Wüstentradition in Sap 10–19* (Beiträge zur Erforschung des Alten Testaments und des antiken Judentums, 32; Frankfurt am Main: Lang, 1993). A study of the use of the biblical text in Wis. 10–19.

Skehan, Patrick W., *Studies in Israelite Poetry and Wisdom* (CBQMS, 1; Washington, DC: Catholic Biblical Association, 1971). This contains a number of studies and reviews relating to the Wisdom of Solomon.

Winston, David, 'Solomon, Wisdom of', *Anchor Bible Dictionary* (ed. D.N. Freedman *et al.*; 6 vols.; New York: Doubleday, 1992): VI, 120-27. A briefer but more recent introduction than his 1979 commentary.

Abbreviations

AB	Anchor Bible
AJSL	*American Journal of Semitic Languages and Literatures*
AnBib	Analecta biblica
ANRW	*Aufstieg und Niedergang der römischen Welt*
BASOR	*Bulletin of the American Schools of Oriental Research*
Bib	*Biblica*
BJS	*Brown Judaic Studies*
CBQ	*Catholic Biblical Quarterly*
CBQMS	*Catholic Biblical Quarterly*, Monograph Series
CRINT	Compendia rerum iudaicarum ad Novum Testamentum
EBib	Etudes bibliques
FRLANT	Forschungen zur Religion und Literatur des Alten und Neuen Testaments
HR	*History of Religions*
HTR	*Harvard Theological Review*
HUCA	*Hebrew Union College Annual*
JBL	Journal of Biblical Literature
JJS	*Journal of Jewish Studies*
JQR	*Jewish Quarterly Review*
JSHRZ	Jüdische Schriften aus hellenistisch-römischer Zeit
JSJ	*Journal for the Study of Judaism in the Persian, Hellenistic and Roman Period*
JSPSup	*Journal for the Study of the Pseudepigrapha*, Supplement Series
MGWJ	*Monatsschrift für Geschichte und Wissenschaft des Judentums*
NJPS	New Jewish Publication Society Translation
OBO	Orbis biblicus et orientalis
SBLDS	SBL Dissertation Series
SBLSBS	SBL Sources for Biblical Study
SBLTT	SBL Texts and Translations
SJLA	Studies in Judaism in Late Antiquity
SNTSMS	Society for New Testament Studies Monograph Series
SUNT	Studien zur Umwelt des Neuen Testaments
TF	*Theologische Forschung*
TU	Texte und Untersuchungen
TZ	*Theologische Zeitschrift*

| *VT* | *Vetus Testamentum* |
| WMANT | Wissenschaftliche Monographien zum Alten und Neuen Testament |

1

INTRODUCTION

It is customary in an introductory treatment to discuss such matters as date, place of composition, and authorship. I do not do that here for several reasons. Most of our knowledge of such things must be gleaned from the book itself; therefore, it is best to begin by looking at the book—at its contents and message—and only then move to questions of authorship. Also, the student should not just accept my word for such matters but should see the process of reasoning and be in a position to make a critical judgment about pronouncements on who wrote the book, and when and where. It is especially important that decisions about the theology and message of the book should not be determined by a priori judgments about time and place of writing.

Contents

The first major section (chs. 1–5) is an address to the 'rulers of the earth' (1.1). It is mainly a discourse on righteousness and wickedness and at times seems to have a sort of miscellaneous character. Nevertheless, there are a number of themes that tend to fall in block sections of chs. 1–5. The 'rulers', who are addressed here, are urged to love righteousness and seek the Lord with sincerity of heart (1.1-5). God knows all and will punish for evil, especially for sins by the mouth (1.6-11). In 1.12-15 the speaker notes that God did not make death and does not delight in it. He created life and existence, without destruction or Hades. The key statement made is that righteousness is immortal (1.15).

Wis. 1.16–2.24 is a discourse on the ungodly and their ways. It seeks to expound the logic of their thought. They think they were born by mere chance and will go into nothing, with no remembrance of them or their works. Therefore, the only thing to do is to enjoy the moment to the full. This leads to a conclusion whose logic might be doubted by modern readers: therefore, the wicked say, let us oppress the righteous because he judges us, and if he is really God's child, God will deliver him. In thinking this, the wicked have deceived themselves, for humanity was created for immortality, not corruption (2.23-24).

The rest of the first major section (3.1–5.23) contrasts the righteous and the wicked. In ch. 3, the souls of the righteous are protected, despite appearances. They are in the hands of God and only seem to have died. The discipline of the righteous is only to refine them. Their final reward is to shine and rule with the Lord. Even if the righteous are barren or eunuchs, they are blessed. On the other hand, the wicked are punished: even their wives are foolish and their children evil. The righteous are in contrast to the offspring of the wicked who gain no benefit even if they live long.

Wis. 4.1-19 continues the same theme. Childlessness with virtue is better than evil offspring (4.1-9). Immortality lies in the memory of virtue. The offspring of the wicked will gain nothing but will be only witnesses to the wickedness of their parents. The death of the righteous is not an evil because they are taken only to protect them from the evil of the world. Age is not measured in the number of years; even if they die early, they are at rest; they are perfected the same as if they had filled long years. The wicked may laugh at the short life of the righteous, but the Lord will laugh at them as they are punished.

Wis. 4.20–5.23 describes the anguish of the wicked in judgment when they see the salvation of the righteous. They will be astonished at the lot of the righteous. Their wealth and arrogance will not help them now; indeed, their repentance will accomplish nothing. They ceased to be as soon as they were born. By contrast, the righteous will live forever, protected from their foes. They will receive a crown and the Lord's whole armor. Nature itself will fight against their foes.

The next major section (chs. 6–9) has the figure of wisdom as its main subject. The speaker is Solomon, and though his identity is never made explicit, it is clearly implied at several points (7.1-6; 9.8). He addresses the mighty of the earth and tells them to learn wisdom (ch. 6). Wisdom is easy to find by those worthy of her (6.12-16). By means of a sorites (see p. 37), 'Solomon' shows that the beginning of wisdom (which is desire for instruction) leads eventually to a kingdom. He will tell how to gain wisdom (6.21-25). The speaker then launches into an autobiographical section (7.1–9.18) which identifies him as Solomon. Wisdom was the answer to prayer and is more important than wealth and honor (7.7-14). God is the ultimate guide and source of knowledge, including skill in crafts and knowledge of nature (7.15-22).

The characteristics of wisdom are now delineated (7.22–8.2); she is a pure emanation from God—a reflection of his light (7.25-26). 'Solomon' loves her for her characteristics and the benefits she can bestow (8.2-16). He loved her like a bride (8.2). Her labors are the four cardinal virtues of moderation, justice, courage, and practical wisdom (see p. 38). If you take her, you will receive all sorts of rewards (8.9-15). Having considered all these benefits, 'Solomon' prays for wisdom because only God can give it (8.17–9.18).

The third major section (chs. 10–19) is a midrash on wisdom's and God's activities in history, from Adam to the conquest of Canaan, with major excursions into the question of idolatry and pagan worship. It begins with a survey of history from Adam to Moses and the exodus, via Cain and Abel, Noah, Abraham, Lot, Jacob, and Joseph (10.1-21). The author begins a midrash on the plagues of Exodus (though it is then interrupted by his excursus on idolatry in 13.1–15.7). These are presented as a series of contrasts or *synkrises* (see pp. 37-38 on this term) in which Israel benefited from the very things which punished their enemies (11.5). Instead of the river turned to blood, because of the attempt of the Egyptians to slay the Israelite infants, Israel received abundant water to quench their thirst in the wilderness (11.6-8). God may discipline his people to teach them, but this is done in mercy and is nothing to be compared with how he punishes the wicked (11.9-14).

The next section has the main subject of punishment, explaining why God did not punish to his full extent initially but only by degrees. Anticipating the attack on false worship to follow in 13–15, the author launches into a long tirade against idolatry and the worship of pagan gods (11.15–12.27). He first of all refers to the worship of irrational animals (11.15-20). God uses the very animals they worship to punish them. It is in God's power to use his great strength, but he is merciful and loves his creation; therefore, he corrects little by little (11.21–12.2). God hated the original inhabitants of the land of Canaan because of their abominable practices, which is why he allowed a worthy colony to replace them; nevertheless, he drove them out gradually to give them the opportunity to repent, despite knowing that they would not change (12.3-11). No one can resist God's strength, but he judges with mildness (12.12-18). He chastises his people to correct them, but their enemies are punished much more (12.19-22). The ungodly went astray after animals as gods; when they suffer through the creatures whom they worship, they will recognize the true God (12.23-27).

He turns to the foolish who marvel at creation but then worship it rather than seeing the God who lies behind it (13.1-9); this leads into the passage on idolatry in which the writer gives a series of examples of its foolishness (13.10–15.17). There is the woodcutter who makes an idol of a castoff piece of wood which has no other value than to be used for firewood (13.11-19). There is the voyager who asks for protection from a piece of wood even flimsier than the ship on which he intends to travel (14.1-7). Cursed are both the idol and the one who made it (14.8-11).

The writer next gives his theory about how idol worship originated (14.12-21), a form of euhemerism (see p. 59). It started by a father's making an image of a beloved child who had died (14.15). Rulers continued the practice by commanding that their images be worshiped, especially by those far from the royal city (14.16-17). Ambitious artisans produced such skillful work that people came to worship the ruler as a god rather than admire him as a man (14.18-21). This idol worship produced all sorts of sins (14.22-31): murder of children, defiling of marriages, adultery, theft, deceit, perjury, and sexual perversion. In contrast, God is kind, patient, and merciful (15.1-6). We acknowledge him and he acknowledges us; we are not deceived by human art. The potters who make images do it for gain and know better (15.7-13). They make gods from the same clay from which they make vessels for base use.

At this point the author returns to the theme of how Israel benefits from the very things used to punish the wicked. The enemies who oppressed God's people thought their idols were gods (15.14-17). They were punished by the very creatures they worshiped and even lost their appetites at such detestable creatures (frogs?), but Israel was shown kindness by being sent quail as food (15.18–16.4). The serpents which plagued Israel were sent as a warning, because God healed them (16.5-14). Their enemies were killed by the bites of locusts and flies, but the Israelite children were not overcome by the bites of serpents. They were healed not by herb or poultice but by God's word (16.12).

Next, nature became the ally of the just: the enemies were punished by fire and water together (16.15-29). The fire burned even in water to destroy the (Egyptian) crops but did not destroy the creatures sent as punishment (flies, etc.). In contrast, God gave his people the food of angels, bread from heaven. Creation works to punish the guilty but is kind to those who trust God that they might learn that they are sustained by God's word rather than crops.

This was followed by the plague of darkness (17.1–18.4). Just when the Egyptians thought the holy people were in their power, they became prisoners of the night, terrified by specters and phantoms. No fire or light could penetrate the darkness, and their magical arts could do nothing. Their wickedness produced cowardice and great fear, which is nothing but giving up the help of reason (17.9-13). People of all occupations were prisoners of this darkness, terrified by every sound (17.14-19). Only they were in darkness, while the rest of the world had light (17.20-21). The Holy Ones (Israelites) had light and could be heard but not seen by the Egyptians (18.1-4). God provided a pillar of fire to guide them. Their enemies, who had tried to imprison them (through whom the light of the law came into the world), deserved to be imprisoned in darkness.

The death of the firstborn was a deserved exchange for trying to kill the infants of the Holy Ones (18.5-25). Their ancestors knew beforehand what was happening and offered sacrifices in secret. The slave had the same punishment as the master. The living were insufficient to bury the dead. They had disbelieved through their magical arts, but now they acknowledged God. God's word leapt from heaven like a stern warrior (18.14-16). The dying had dreams which told them why they suffered (18.17-19). Death also came to the righteous but did not long continue (18.20-25). A blameless man (Aaron) propitiated with incense, prevailing not by force of arms but by God's word. The whole world was depicted on his (priestly) robes and God's majesty on his head; he was able to force back the Destroyer.

Driven by continuing anger, the Egyptians pursued the Israelites, God knowing in advance their future actions (19.1-12). They changed their minds even while mourning in order that their punishment might be full. But creation itself cooperated to bring them safely through the sea, and they rejoiced at quail for food, remembering the recent plagues of gnats and frogs. These punishments did not come without prior signs (19.13). Just as (Lot's) guests were mistreated, so the Egyptians mistreated the Israelites who were their guests (19.14-17). The elements changed roles: land animals became water creatures and vice versa; fire burned in water but failed to consume flesh or heavenly food (manna).

The last vese is a concluding doxology which summarizes what God was intending in 11–19: in everything you have exalted your people, O Lord (19.22).

Structure

Already in the days before form criticism, attempts were made to divide
up the book by theme. In the past half century a great deal has been
done by the application of the principles of form criticism. A number of
rhetorical devices have helped to clarify the structure of the book. Some
of these can be outlined here. One of the major features is that of *parallelism*, a feature not confined to literature in one language but found in
Greek and Hebrew literature as well as others. This can be as simple as
parallel stichs (poetic lines) in a verse but larger structures also often have
parallel sections. This parallelism may be linear in nature, but a frequent
form is that known as *chiasm* or concentric parallelism. This is named
after the Greek letter *chi* (χ), which is similar in shape to the x of the
Latin alphabet. In this form, the first set of structures are paralleled by a
second set in reverse order: that is, the elements a b c d e are matched
by a parallel set of elements in the order e′ d′ c′ b′ a′.

Much of the work on the Wisdom of Solomon in the past few
decades has focused on the question of parallel structures within major
sections rather than a new delineation of the main sections themselves.
The major divisions of the book have not changed substantially since
the nineteenth century:

> 1–5: Book of Eschatology
> 6–9: Book of Wisdom
> 10–19: Book of History

There remains some question about the limits of these books, and a
number of scholars have recently argued for the division 1–6, 7–10,
11–19. Also, some scholars have wanted to divide the book into four
sections by splitting the last book into two. For example, Reese (1970:
91-102, 114-16) would make 11.15–15.19 a separate book. This material was long ago recognized to be a digression, so whether one considers it a separate book (to make the last section into two books: Book
of History 11.1-14 + 16–19; Book of Divine Justice and Human Folly
11.15–15.19) or simply as a digression in one book is really a minor
point.

One of the fundamental problems is how to decide the limits of a
unit. Modern authors use various stylistic indications to signpost their
organization: paragraphs, headings, chapter divisions, tables of contents,
and the like. Ancient writings might be written in a continuous text
without divisions—indeed, even without divisions between words in

many Greek manuscripts. So the reader had to pick up the author's intent by linguistic clues. One of those frequently used is the *inclusio* or inclusion. This is very simple. The section is marked off by having the beginning and the end of a section use the same device. This can be a particular word or words, a phrase, a sentence, or even a subject. Examples will be given below. The present consensus about the structure of the book depends heavily on the work of J.M. Reese and A.G. Wright. Reese demonstrated 'a) the use of the inclusion as a means of delimiting units, b) the use of parallelism in constructing concentric or parallel structures, c) the use of flashbacks to link various units' (Kolarcik 1991: 13-14). Wright developed Reese's scheme further, and much follow-up work has been done by Gilbert, Kolarcik, and others. What they have shown is the extent of parallelism, especially concentric parallelism, in the Wisdom of Solomon.

The extent of the first section (the Book of Eschatology) depends on how one interprets the address to the kings in 6.1. Since 1.1 begins with an address to the judges of the earth, it is often thought that 6.1 begins a new section. However, several recent interpreters see it as an *inclusio*, so that 6.1-21 does not start a new section but completes the Book of Eschatology. If this is accepted, 1.1–6.21 seems to exhibit a concentric structure (cf. Reese 1965: 394-96; Wright 1967a: 168-73; Kolarcik 1991: 29-62);

A Address to judges: exhortation to justice	1.1-15
B Speech of the wicked	1.16–2.24
C Four diptychs contrasting the just and wicked	3.1–4.20
B′ Speech of the wicked	5.1-23
A′ Address to kings: exhortation to wisdom	6.1-21

Section C forms a twofold structure. It consists of four parts, each of which contrasts the righteous and wicked: 3.1-12; 3.13-19; 4.1-6; 4.7-20. In addition, it is broken up into three parts by inclusions which show a progressive punishment on the wicked:

> 3.1-12 suffering (*inclusio* marked by *aphrōn* 'foolish' in 3.2, 12)
> 3.13–4.6 childlessness (*karpos* 'fruit', 3.13, 4.5)
> 4.7-20 early death (*timion* 'honourable' 4.8, *atimon* 'dishonourable' 4.19)

In the middle section (the Book of Wisdom) chs. 7–8 also seem to exhibit a concentric structure (Wright 1967a: 168, 173-74):

A Birth of Solomon	7.1-6
B Solomon asks for wisdom from God	7.7-12
C Also given wealth and power	7.13-22
D Description of wisdom	7.22b–8.1
C′ Wisdom brings all good things	8.2-8
B′ Solomon great king through wisdom	8.9-16
A′ Wisdom only available by prayer	8.17-21

Chapter 9 has a separate structure which, according to Gilbert (1970), has a concentric parallelism extending down to the level of the individual verses. This is based on a detailed study of the Greek wording and is not easily summarized in English translation, but his scheme is as follows:

```
A 1-3
    B 4
        C 5-6
            D 7-8
                E 9
                    F 10ab
                E′ 10c-11
            D′ 12
        C′ 13-17aα
    B′ 17aβb
A′ 18
```

Even C′ forms its own concentric structure:

```
A 13
    B 14
        C 15
    B′ 16ab
```

A′ 16c-17aα

This analysis may appear to be overly complicated and also overly confident. Readers are right to be cautious, for Gilbert himself emphasizes a threefold structure in other writings (1984: 303; 1986: 71):

A Mankind in general	9.1-6
B Solomon	9.7-12
A′ Mankind	9.13-18

Also, Wright (1967a: 174) gives a different analysis which sees parallel symmetry rather than concentric:

A Address, petition, motive	9.1-5
B General observation	9.6
A′ Address, petition, motive	9.7-12
B′ General observation	9.13-18

This illustrates that literary structures do not distill into the scholar's notebook like a chemical precipitant in a test-tube—there is necessarily a subjective element in the structural analyses offered by scholars, and what seems crystal clear to one scholar is highly dubious to another.

The final section (the Book of History) begins with a transitional chapter (10). Chapters 11–19 have a particular structure around a series of antitheses, but they are made complicated with the two digressions in 11.15–15.17 which have their own structure. If we leave out the digressions, as is universally done, there are still two possible analyses of these chapters. One is to see seven antitheses, drawing on six of the plagues plus the destruction of the Egyptian army in the Red Sea. This goes back as early as Focke (Focke 1913: 13; cf. Reese 1965; Gilbert 1984: 305; 1986: 73-74):

First: Nile into blood//water from the rock	11.4-14
Second: small animals//quail	16.1-4
Third: locusts and flies//healing from serpents	16.5-14
Fourth: hail//manna	16.15–17.1
Fifth: darkness//pillar of fire	17.2–18.4
Sixth: death of the firstborn//Israelites preserved	18.5-25
Seventh: death in the Red Sea//Israelites pass unharmed	19.1-13

A number of recent researchers argue for only five antitheses or diptychs, however; this is because of internal indications as to structure (Wright 1965; cf. Gilbert 1984: 305; 1986: 73-74). Four of the five are introduced by the Greek word *anti* 'against, opposite' (11.6; 16.2, 20; 18.3). The last describes only one event (the death of the Egyptians) with two results (the death of the firstborn and the destruction of the Egyptian army). It is the formal structure rather than just the content which argues for this analysis.

The two digressions have their own internal structure. 11.15–12.27 discusses the question of why God punished the Egyptians the way he did. The answer given is that he was punishing by degrees so that the sinners would have an opportunity to repent. This has two parallel sections (Gilbert 1984: 306; 1986: 73-74): 11.15–12.2 describes what happened to the Egyptians, while 12.3-18 describes what happened to the Canaanites. The author then draws the lesson for Israel (12.19-22) before reverting to the account of the plagues (12.23-27). The second digression on false worship can be said to exhibit two structures, each with its own integrity (Gilbert 1984: 306; 1986: 74-75). According to content, the following progression of worship and also blame is evident:

Worship of natural world//philosophers incur least blame	13.1-9
Worship of idols//idolators more strongly condemned	13.10–15.13
Worship of animals//Egyptians worst of all	15.14-19

As far as formal structure is concerned, once again a concentric pattern seems evident:

A Idols of gold, silver, stone, wood + carpenter	13.10-19
B Invocation to God; salvation history; transition	14.1-10
C Punishment of idols; invention of idolatry; punishment of idolators	14.11-31
B´ Invocation to God; salvation history; transition	15.1-6
A´ Idols of clay + potter	15.7-13

The following structure is a synthesis of some of the main recent studies. This does not mean that any one researcher would agree with it. In any case, it is not meant to be definitive but only illustrative; it serves to demonstrate the sort of analysis to which the book is susceptible:

I. The Book of Eschatology	1.1–6.21
A Exhortation to justice	1.1-15
B Speech of the impious	1.16–2.24
C Four diptychs contrasting the just and the wicked	3.1–4.20
B´ Speech of the impious	5.1-23
A´ Exhortation to wisdom	6.1-21
II. The Book of Wisdom	6.22–11.1
A Introduction	6.22-25
B Solomon's speech	7.1–8.21
a Solomon's birth	7.1-6
b Solomon asks for wisdom from God	7.7-12
c Given wealth and power	7.13-22
d Description of wisdom	7.22b–8.1
c´ Wisdom brings all good things	8.2-8
b´ Solomon becomes great through wisdom	8.9-16
a´ Wisdom is available only by prayer	8.17-21
C Solomon's prayer	9.1-18
a Address, petition, motive	9.1-5
b General observation	9.6
a´ Address, petition, motive	9.7-12
b´ General observation	9.13-18
D Transition to part III	10.1–11.1
III. The Book of History	11.2–19.22
A Introduction	11.2-5
B Five antithetical diptychs	11.6–19.21
a Plague of Nile//water from the rock	11.6-14
b Plague of small animals (broken off)	11.15-16

Some scholars have also suggested that the book was designed arithmetically. Patrick Skehan (1945) claimed to count 500 stichs (poetic lines) in 1–9; chapter 10 would be a transition, with 60 stichs; and 11–19 have 560 stichs for a total of 1120 stichs. The problem is that the number of stichs varies in the manuscripts between 1000 and 1250. Simply taking a rough mean, as Skehan does, is arbitrary. Skehan himself evidently came to the same conclusion, for when his article was reprinted (1971: 132-36) this section was omitted.

More promising is a suggestion of A.G. Wright's (1976b). He argues that the book is based on the Golden Mean of classical antiquity. This is a mathematical ratio regarded as an ideal proportion; it was expressed in architecture (e.g., in the construction of the Parthenon) as a relationship between the height and width of a building. It is based on a sophisticated mathematical formula, however, in which the Golden Mean is calculated by means of a series in which a number equals the sum of the previous two numbers in the series $(x/y/x+y/y+x+y/...)$. In finding the Golden Mean formula in the book, Wright counts verses (rather than stichs): 138 in Wis. 1.1–6.21; 222 in Wis. 1.1–9.1; and if the digressions (11.15–15.17) are omitted, Wis. 11–19 contains 138. Wis. 1.1–9.1 and 11–19 together total 360 verses. Thus, 138/222/360 (138 + 222 = 360) is a part of the mathematical series of the Golden Mean. Wright points to a total of 21 examples of the Golden Mean in the book. The evidence is very impressive, but not everyone is convinced (Gilbert 1986: 89).

On the question of 'flashbacks', see the next section.

Unity of the Book

The question of the unity of the Wisdom of Solomon—whether by a single author or several—is very much tied up with discussion of the structure. A unified structure is often used as an argument for single authorship, and this can be a powerful argument if there is agreement among scholars about its unity; however, unity of structure can also be achieved by careful editing, so this by itself cannot be conclusive. In the past couple of centuries a number of well-known scholars have argued that certain parts of the book were not from the same hand. This view has closely accompanied the assumption that certain parts of the book had a Semitic original (pp. 32-33). Nevertheless, recent scholarship has generally favored the unity of the work. Some of the reasons are the following (cf. Gilbert 1986: 88-91):

1. There is no evidence of a Hebrew or Aramaic text for the book or any part of it, and the hypotheses which propose such have not met with wide acceptance (pp. 32-33).

2. The concentric structure found throughout the work (pp. 18-23) argues for a single author. Although there is not an overall concentric structure for the entire work, the concentric parallelism found in the various parts suggests a planned writing by a single author.

3. The vocabulary and linguistic style have been taken to suggest a single author (pp. 35-36).

4. The arguments from stichometry have not been convincing, but the endeavor to find evidence of the Golden Mean in the structure have met with greater approval (see p. 23). If this argument is found convincing, it seems a powerful argument in favor of a unified work.

5. The presence of 'flashbacks' is a device suggesting unity of plan in the book (Reese 1970: 122-45). A flashback is 'a short repetition of a significant word or group of words or distinctive idea in two different parts of' the work in question (Reese 1970: 124). Reese lists 45 examples connecting all parts of the book. Although individual examples may be challenged, the cumulative effect is strong: 'This use of flashbacks, which is sustained throughout the entire work, offers a strong literary argument for a single author. Despite a wide range of interests, a unity of outlook and interest underlies all the sections' (Reese 1970: 140).

6.   Themes can be found spanning the different sections of the book (Gilbert 1986: 90-91; Reese 1970: 140-45). Some of these are stronger than others. Two especially important ones are the religious knowledge of God and the theological concept of 'seeing'.

Probably none of these arguments is conclusive by itself. Finding the Golden Mean, so striking at first blush, is treated with skepticism by some. A number of the points could be due to careful editing, even if unified authorship is more likely to produce them: flashbacks could be created by later writers using earlier sections; themes may be the result of editors; the concentric structures found in individual units would still exist if simply added to other literary units, and so on. Yet there is a cumulative effect, and while no argument clinches the matter, unity of authorship seems the most likely conclusion in the light of current knowledge.

Genre

The Wisdom of Solomon has elements in common with many Jewish, ancient Near Eastern, and classical literatures. For example, the themes of gaining wisdom and the activities of Lady Wisdom are well known from the book of Proverbs (see Chapter 4). Parallels to many passages occur equally in the book of Ben Sira. Many of the ancient Near Eastern instructions, from both Egypt and Mesopotamia, emphasize how important it is for young people to acquire wisdom since wisdom is not normally associated with youth and inexperience. The admonitions on obedience and the law remind one of Deuteronomy and also many prophetic passages (some of which are regularly labeled 'deuteronomistic'). The midrash on biblical history in 10–19 is based on Genesis and Exodus. On the other hand, the book is permeated with elements familiar from Greek literature and philosophy (cf. pp. 35-38).

By focusing on only one or other aspect of the book, one could make a case for a variety of literary genres for the book. The Wisdom of Solomon is clearly a wisdom book and to be grouped with Proverbs, Job, Qohelet (Ecclesiastes), and Ben Sira (Ecclesiasticus) as one of only five wisdom books among ancient Jewish literature.

Two main genres have been suggested for the entire book by recent scholars. One is that of the encomium, first proposed by Beauchamp and expounded at greatest length by Gilbert (1984; 1986). The other is that of the Greek genre of the 'exhortatory discourse' (*logos protreptikos* or, in Latin, *logos protrepticus*). It was first proposed by Focke (1913) and subsequently followed by Reese (1970: 117-21) and Winston (1979: 18-20).

The protreptic was apparently first defined and discussed by Aristotle in his work entitled *Protrepticus*. The writing was lost already in antiquity, but it was used as the basis of Cicero's philosophical dialogue *Hortensius*, and modern scholars have attempted to reconstruct it from Cicero and other sources (Düring 1961). It is the reconstructed protreptic from Aristotle that seems to serve as the model for discussing the genre.

The aim of the *logos protreptikos* was to persuade or convince others of a particular course of action. This could be done in one of two ways: (a) by demonstrative logic or (b) by rhetoric. In ancient Athens a group of individuals, usually non-Athenians, sought to teach success for money. These were the so-called Sophists. Although they were in many ways the first private tutors, the scholars, and the university professors, they were pilloried by Socrates and Plato and have become a byword for clever but empty rhetoric. As usual, things were more complicated than presented by Plato, and the caricature of Socrates himself as a Sophist in Aristophanes' *The Clouds* had more than a grain of truth. It is indeed true that one of the main themes of Sophist teaching was the use of rhetoric for purposes of argument and persuasion. Yet Aristotle, himself a pupil of Plato, wrote a treatise on rhetoric, and rhetoric became one of the mainstays of Greek and then Roman education.

Reese summarizes the interpretation that the work is a *logos protreptikos* in the following way:

> In conclusion then, his method of teaching follows the didactic method of the protreptic genre. He develops his religious appeals and moral warnings according to the techniques employed by hellenistic rhetoricians, who taught that exhortations must appeal not only to the intellect but to the other human faculties as well. In all parts of his book, with artistic skill, oratorical beauty, and a wealth of literary allusions, the Sage wished to accomplish the purpose of protreptic literature, that is, 'to arouse an attitude that is esentially active.'

The encomium was also first defined by Aristotle. In his *Rhetoric*, he divided discourses or speeches into three types: the demonstrative, the forensic, and the epideictic. The third was not primarily aimed at persuasion on a course of action but at persuading listeners to admire someone or something. (However, if the admired thing was a value of some sort, the praise would have the ultimate aim of convincing one to adopt it.)

According to this proposal, the Wisdom of Solomon corresponds to the characteristics of the encomium in the following way:

> Exordium (introduction): Wisdom 1–6
> Encomium proper: Wisdom 6–9
> *Synkrisis* (comparison): Wis. 10.1–19.9
> Epilogue and conclusion: Wis. 19.10-22

The book of Wisdom has much in common with the *diatribe*. The Hellenistic diatribe was a specific rhetorical form and should not be confused with our English word 'diatribe'. It was essentially a moral discourse and was much favored by the philosophical street preachers among the Cynics and Stoics, though recent study has emphasized its home in an academic context (Sowers 1981). Its aim was to convince the hearers of a particular course of action, and it always had a moral theme. A good deal of debate about the diatribe has taken place in the past century, and despite disagreements over many issues, there is some consensus that certain diatribes or parts of diatribes have been preserved (e.g., Epictetus, Musonius Rufus, Seneca; see Sowers 1981: 50-78).

A variety of rhetorical devices were used to make the diatribe effective, especially a real or imaginary dialogue with the hearers in which (real or imagined) objections were answered. A common device was to address the hearers directly, by an apostrophe. This is done in Wis. 6.1-2:

> Listen therefore, O kings, and understand;
> learn, O judges of the ends of the earth.
> Give ear, you that rule over multitudes,
> and boast of many nations.

On the other hand, Sowers (1981: 40-41) has criticized Reese for classifying parts of the Wisdom of Solomon as diatribe and will concede only that there is influence from diatribe (see Winston 1979: 20 for a list of diatribal features). It is difficult to find any part of Wisdom of Solomon which exhibits the main feature of the diatribe, dialogue form, though ch. 2 does contain an imaginary speech of an adversary.

The autobiographical narrative is another rhetorical form of potential value for understanding the book. In 7–9 the writer in the person of Solomon describes his life and quest for wisdom. He shows his common humanity with the hearers, despite being a king (7.1-6), but the emphasis is on how he sought out wisdom because of the benefits she is able to bestow. This serves the dual function of gaining the empathy of the hearers and also commending to them the same quest for wisdom.

A favorite device of the Wisdom of Solomon is to contrast two opposites, one considered good and the other bad. Wisdom 1–3 are a contrast of the righteous and the wicked. Here the author has to overcome the common perception that there is no advantage to being righteous, and that wickedness has obvious attractions. To do so he has to show that surface appearances are deceptive. In 10–19 he makes use of a formal *synkrisis* or comparison, as discussed further on pp. 37-38. The contrast in this case is between the sufferings of the Egyptians in the plagues and the blessings bestowed by God on the Israelites.

Another feature of the diatribe is the use of satire and the satirical devices of irony or sarcasm to denounce the rejected alternative ways of living. The Wisdom of Solomon uses this in discussing the use of idols and animal images in worship. The writer is not particularly original in his choice of imagery and does not in fact go beyond earlier Jewish denunciations which can be found already in the book of Jeremiah. He pictures the man who takes a piece of wood, makes a household utensil from it, uses part of it to cook his meal, and then from the most useless remnant makes an idol. Similarly, the potter uses clay to make both a common vessel and an image for worship. Comparable comments are made about the worship of deities pictured in the form of animals. It may not be an outstanding example of satire, but it no doubt served its purpose.

Place in the Canon

There is no evidence that the Wisdom of Solomon ever had canonical status in any Jewish group. As with a number of Jewish writings from antiquity, all our textual and other data come via the Christian tradition. No evidence of the work is found at Qumran. The ascription of the work to Solomon may suggest that the writer intended it to be taken as a genuine work from the ancient sage, but whether any Jews treated it that way is unknown.

The work was early accepted as of equal status with other Old Testament books by some Christian writers. Some scholars have argued that it is already quoted by New Testament writers, but this is debatable. Although some passages of the Wisdom of Solomon are similar to some New Testament verses, there is no clear quotation, and writers such as Paul may have been drawing on common Jewish tradition (cf. Larcher 1969: 11-30, 36-41). It seems to be known by Clement of Rome writing about 110 CE (27.5//Wis. 12.12; 11.21; cf. also 60.1 //Wis. 7.17). It was perhaps used by Ignatius and may be quoted by other second-century writers but this is not certain (Larcher 1969: 36-38). The Wisdom of Solomon is certainly used as Scripture by such early-third-century writers as Tertullian and Clement of Alexandria, and in pseudo-Hippolytus's *Remonstratio adversus Judaeos*. On the other hand, its canonicity was doubted by Origen (*Contra Celsum* 5.29; *De Principiis* 4.4.6[33]), though he sometimes quotes as it as canonical (*De Principiis* 1.2.5-13). Jerome was dubious about the deuterocanonical books because they did not exist in the Hebrew canon of his time. The book became a part of the Roman Catholic and Greek Orthodox canons but is normally excluded from the canons of most Protestant groups.

Further Reading

The structure of the work is discussed in recent commentaries, but much of the detailed work is to be found in important individual studies which include the following: Gilbert (1970: 301-31); Kolarcik (1991); Reese (1965: 391-99; 1970); Skehan (1945: 1-12; 1971); Wright (1965: 28-34; 1967a: 165-84; 1967b: 524-38).

On the genre of the book, see Düring (1961); Gilbert (1986: 11.65-77); Reese (1970: 117-21); Winston (1979).

On the Hellenistic diatribe, see Sowers (1981, especially the survey on 7-78).

The subject of canonical literature is complicated; see Grant (1966: 1.462-72).

2

TYPOLOGY, MIDRASH, AND GREEK RHETORIC

Introduction

Biblical interpretation arose as soon as certain writings began to acquire authoritative status. It has been argued that this process can be discerned even within the biblical literature itself. Commentary is certainly already to be discovered here and there in the Greek translation of the Hebrew Bible, the Septuagint. Explicit commentary on some parts of the Old Testament from an early time can be found among the Qumran scrolls and also in other Jewish writings of the Second Temple period. This includes Greek writings which now survive only in fragments, such as Aristobulus and Ezekiel the Tragedian.

A variety of terms have been used with regard to the different sorts of biblical interpretation known to us in antiquity. The term 'midrash' is widely used, but with a bewildering variety of meanings. It will be used here in its more original sense in Jewish literature, as discussed below. Other types of interpretation, such as 'allegory' and 'typology', are not unknown in Jewish writings, but their use tends to be limited in literature in Hebrew and Aramaic until a rather later time. That is, it is mainly in Jewish literature in Greek that their developed use is first and most widely found, parallel to the use of allegory in certain interpretations of Homer and other Greek traditional literature.

It was once widely believed in biblical theology that a sharp contrast between the Hebrew/Jewish and the Greek could and should be made. This was often expressed as 'Hebrew thought', in contrast to 'Greek thought'. The former was viewed positively; and the latter, negatively. Hebrew thought was dynamic and expressed in verbs, whereas Greek thought was static, expressed in nouns. Strangely, the New Testament—written in Greek—was characterized as embodying *Hebrew* thought. This view was subjected to a devastating critique by James Barr and has since been widely abandoned in mainstream scholarship. However, it continues to surface periodically, especially in writings aimed at the general reader. There is also still a widespread undercurrent even in scholarship which sees Hellenization and Judaism as incompatible, even conflicting, entities. On this basis, some point to Greek influence on Philo and the author of the Wisdom of Solomon whom they then treat negatively; others, viewing their works positively, seek to disassociate them from such influence.

Much recent specialist study has been more balanced. From the time of Alexander to the Arab conquest, much of the ancient Near East came under Greek domination. A new cultural entity was created which was neither Greek nor Near Eastern but a complex synthesis known as Hellenization. Many of the institutions of the old Near Eastern empires continued. Much of the administrative structure of the Ptolemaic and Seleucid empires was taken over from the Babylonian, Persian, and Egyptian rule of the past. The people in the lower strata of society continued to live much as they had for centuries. But many Greek elements also entered society at various points. They were most evident in the royal courts and among the upper levels of society, both those of Greek descent and those of the natives. Greek cities were founded, initially colonized by descendents of Alexander's soldiers. But as time went on, some of the original Oriental cities obtained permission to become Greek cities, with a Greek form of civic government. Their citizens practiced certain customs borrowed mainly from the Greeks, and the young men were given a traditional Greek education to prepare them for citizenship.

The effect on the Jews varied considerably. In the area of religion, our extant sources indicate few Jews abandoned their religion or adopted pagan forms of worship—but then few other Near Eastern peoples abandoned their traditional religion for Greek worship, either. No attempt was made to change traditional forms of religion among the native peoples. However, many Jews were settled in Greek-speaking areas and came in contact with Greek knowledge and education. The majority of Jews were not a part of the upper class and did not have the opportunity to study Greek literature, but there were exceptions. The family of Philo of Alexandria, for example, was extremely wealthy and influential not only in the Jewish community but in the Roman empire at large, consorting with Roman nobles and even kings. Philo was well-versed in knowledge imparted by the traditional Greek education and occasionally speaks of experiences such as attending dramas and the spectacles in the arena. He wrote in a good educated Hellenistic style, and from all indications Greek was his first language. He knew little or no Hebrew, and his Bible was the Septuagint, the translation of the Hebrew Scriptures into Greek.

Not many Jews had Philo's education, background, and privileges, but many of them knew Greek—sometimes in addition to other languages but sometimes even as their first or main or even only language. A body of Jewish literature in the Greek language began to grow. Some of this consisted of writings originally written in Hebrew or Aramaic but then translated into Greek; other works were evidently composed in Greek from the beginning. In some cases, their writers were very knowledgeable in Greek literature and made use of literary allusions, literary and rhetorical devices, and references to philosophical concepts. One such writer is Philo. Another is the author of the Wisdom of Solomon.

The Original Text

The text of the Wisdom of Solomon has come down to us in Greek. A few papyrus fragments go back as early as the third century CE. The main witnesses are the great uncials of the fourth century, Vaticanus (B) and Sinaiticus (‭א‬); and of the fifth century, Alexandrinus (A). There is also the Old Latin version, generally recognized to be translated from the Greek. Jerome did not make a new translation for the Vulgate but only edited a version of the Old Latin. There is also a Syriac (Aramaic) version as well, but it is also a translation from Greek. The linguistic evidence up to 1961 is available in the definitive edition of Ziegler. He gives an eclectic text, though scholars may well differ from him in individual readings. See the Preface for the various text editions.

The question of the original language and even of the unity of the book has been much debated in the past couple of centuries or so. There is no evidence of a Hebrew version in antiquity. It is primarily in modern scholarship that a Hebrew or even Aramaic original has been proposed for part or all of the book. The difficulty is that the book shows little evidence of being translation Greek. Translation Greek style is well known from the Septuagint translation. It is clear that the author of the Wisdom of Solomon knew the Bible in its Septuagint form, but his style is quite different and does not generally show the characteristics associated with works translated from a Semitic original. Most Jewish books translated from Semitic originals are easily identified. It is true that occasionally it is difficult to know whether a book is a translation or originally composed in 'Jewish Greek', but the Wisdom of Solomon is plainly distinguished from writings such as these.

Several arguments have been advanced to attempt to demonstrate a Semitic background. The article by F. Zimmerman (1966-67) can be used as an instance of those used. For example, the sorites in Wis. 6.17-20 has been taken as evidence because it is a literary form well attested in Tannaitic literature such as the Mishnah. However, H.A. Fischel (1973) has demonstrated that the Tannaim usage is a borrowing from the Greco–Roman milieu (see p. 37). Zimmerman's other arguments are based on alleged wordplays and mistranslations. Scholars have generally not found these convincing. The unity of the book can be a separate question from that of the original language, but those who propose a Semitic original for only certain sections usually also suggest multiple authorship.

For further evidence of the Greek style of the book, see pp. 35-38 below.

Allegory and Typology

The time and place of the Wisdom of Solomon's composition will be discussed in the last chapter. At the moment, we must allow for several possible contexts. In some Jewish writings allegory is the main form of interpretation, as in Philo of Alexandria and in the extant portions of Aristobulus. The question of how widespread allegorical interpretation was among the Jews at the time is debated, and some have even proposed the existence of 'an Old Palestinian allegorical exegesis'. This proposal does not stand up to close examination and, in fact, the main roots of Philonic allegory are from Greek allegorical exegesis (Grabbe 1988: 66-87). This particular point need not be explored further, however, since there seems to be almost no allegorizing in the Wisdom of Solomon even if it might have been widespread in its literary context.

There is a hint, however, that the writer knew and approved of at least one allegory toward the end of the book. In a narrative about Aaron, the author of the Wisdom of Solomon makes a brief reference to the priestly attire (18.24):

> For on his long robe the whole world was depicted,
> and the glories of the ancestors were engraved on the four rows of stones,
> and your majesty was on the diadem upon his head.

This a rather obscure statement in context and is not further elucidated, but a tradition about the various parts of the high priestly dress being symbolic of the universe is found in several other writers. For example, Josephus writes (*Ant.* 3.7.7 §§184-87):

> The high-priest's tunic likewise signifies the earth being of linen, and its blue the arch of heaven, while it recalls the lightnings by its pomegranates, the thunder by the sound of its bells. His upper garment, too, denotes universal nature, which it pleased God to make of four elements; being further inter-woven with gold in token, I imagine, of the all-pervading sunlight. The *essên* [breastplate], again, he set in the midst of the garment, after the manner of the earth, which occupies the midmost place; and by the girdle wherewith he encompassed it he signified the ocean, which holds the whole in its embrace. Sun and moon are indicated by the two sardonyxes wherewith he pinned the high-priest's robe. As for the twelve stones, whether one would prefer to read in them the months or the constellations of like number, which the Greeks call the circle of the zodiac, he will not mistake the lawgiver's inten-tion. Furthermore the head-dress appears to me to symbolize heaven, being blue; else it would not have borne upon it the name of God, blazoned upon the crown—a crown, moreover, of gold by reason of that sheen in which the Deity most delights.

Similarly, Philo writes on the meaning of the high priestly robes at even greater length (*Vit. Mos.* 2.117-26). Again, there is 'in it as a whole and in its parts a typical representation of the world and its particular parts' (2.117). The robe is the atmosphere and air. The earth is repre-sented by the flowers at the ankles, and water by the pomegranates. These three elements represent life since all living things come from and exist in them. The ephod is a symbol of heaven, with the stones on the shoulder piece representing the sun and moon or the two hemispheres of the sky. The twelve stones are the signs of the zodiac.

Even though an allegory may be alluded to, the nearest thing to an actual allegory is the passage on God's armor in a passage reminiscent of Eph. 6.14-17 but certainly earlier (5.17-20):

> The Lord will take his zeal as his whole armor,
> and will arm all creation to repel his enemies;
> he will put on righteousness as a breastplate,
> and wear impartial justice as a helmet;
> he will take holiness as an invincible shield,
> and sharpen stern wrath for a sword,
> and creation will join with him to fight against his frenzied foes.

Typology might seem to be more promising than allegory as an interpretative device. Typology and allegory have much in common, but
typology need not rise to full-blown allegory. The question is not one
of whether typology might be 'better' theologically than allegory, a
proposition which can hardly be sustained (Barr 1966: 103-48), but
rather the specific form of biblical interpretation used by the Wisdom
of Solomon.

It seems that in the Book of History (chs. 10–19), the righteous and
wicked of the Book of Eschatology (chs. 1–5) are symbolized by the
Israelites and Egyptians. This is typology, but very little else in the book
seems to fit into this category. The potential is there, but the writer does
not seem to make use of it. Reese has no hesitation in speaking of
typology: 'His method was not that of allegory used later by Philo, but
rather that of typology' (Reese 1970: 160). Reese also notes that
Solomon is 'the type of everyman' (1970: 76), but otherwise he does
not develop the concept. The term 'type' (Greek *tupos*) is not used in
the book, and there is danger of reading into the work something not
intended by the author. Unless better evidence can be found, typology
as form of intepretation in the book should probably be accepted only
with caution.

Greek Rhetoric

The contribution to the Wisdom of Solomon from the Greek side is
readily apparent throughout the book and would have been recognized
by non-Jewish Greek speakers. The book is written in a good Greek
style that 'manifests the influence of training in Greek rhetoric' (Reese
1970: 3). A study of the vocabulary of the the Wisdom of Solomon
shows that many words are not found elsewhere in the Septuagint
version, and that vocabulary shared with other Septuagintal books often
has a different connotation, usually that better known from educated
classical or Hellenistic usage (Reese 1970: 1-24). The vocabulary used in
the Wisdom of Solomon but not elsewhere in the Septuagint tends to
fall under four headings or fields of vocabulary: (a) religious; (b) philosophical; (c) ethical; (d) psychological. Only some examples can be
given here, and Reese should be seen for further details and secondary
literature.

The Wisdom of Solomon uses several words well-known from Hellenistic cultic vocabulary. For whatever reason, the author found them
useful for his purposes. There are several possible purposes to his usage,

but two of them seem to be the following: first, they are words which would have had meaning to anyone familiar with the Hellenistic cults and religions; secondly, in the case of his discussion of idols he seems to use this vocabulary (e.g., *anōnuma* 'unspeakable' and *apsucha* 'lifeless') as a weapon. He uses vocabulary from the Greek mystery cults (e.g., *mustai* 'initiates' and *splagchnophagos thoina* 'sacrificial dining') to condemn the alleged practices of the Canaanites (12.5).

A good example of a passage in which the author demonstates his knowledge of the Hellenistic tradition is the 'philosophical presentation' of Wis. 13.1-9 (Reese 1970: 50-62). As noted at pp. 21-22, this is part of a threefold progression about the different sorts of false worship, this being the least offensive—that of nature worship. The author is attempting to show that the material philosophers have no excuse for worshiping the creation rather than the creator. In so doing, he uses a Hellenistic philosophical argument, expressed in the Greek literary form of the period, in aid of his aim which is thoroughly within Judaism. Reese notes six areas showing the influence of philosophy (1970: 52-62):

(1) Wis. 13.1 uses the expression 'the one who is' (*ho ōn*). This is used of the Supreme Being by the Platonists as well as by the Septuagint in Exod. 3.14, but the senses are somewhat different. The Greek translator of Exodus uses the term to refer to the one and only God, whereas in Platonic philosophy the supreme being was separate from the creator of the universe, which leads to the next point.

(2) God as the Supreme Being is also the creator (13.1: *technitēs*). He is not a part of nature but is its originator.

(3) Wis. 13.1 also speaks of the ignorance of God on the part of these educated individuals. In Hellenistic literature the expression often has the meaning 'impiety'.

(4) The elements worshiped are enumerated in Wis. 13.2 (cf. also at pp. 42-43 below). Associated with them are a number of philosophical terms; for example, the phrase 'moderators of the world' (*prutaneis tou kosmou*) seems to be a reference to 'astral piety'. Another technical philosophical expression is 'power and effect' (13.4: *dunamis kai energeia*).

(5) The type of argumentation in 13.5 is Hellenistic, not biblical. It includes the common Hellenistic form of reasoning from analogy, and it argues that the beauty of the creation requires some overseer and source of beauty behind it.

(6)   Aeon speculation. The Greek term *aiōn* could mean both 'world' and 'age', but in Hellenistic speculation it was used of a mystical religio–philosophical concept: 'the personified cosmic God and the entire limitless world and infinite time', 'a kind of world-soul exercising its power over the movements of the cosmos and giving all things existence' (Reese 1970: 58-59). The author of the Wisdom of Solomon (13.9) attacks the speculation of the philosophers in this area, showing that he understood its significance for them.

This short passage (13.1-9) is a prime example of how the author knows and uses a good Hellenistic education in the service of his religious aims. Although he freely draws on the biblical tradition, he is by no means limited to it. Greek literature and rhetoric are a full part of his arsenal. As Reese states, 'It is inconceivable that he could have formulated this judgment without being acquainted with contemporary philosophical speculation' (1970: 57).

Several literary forms best known from Greek literature are used in the Wisdom of Solomon. One of these is in 6.17-20:

> The beginning of wisdom is the most sincere desire for instruction,
> and concern for instruction is love of her,
> and love of her is the keeping of her laws,
> and giving heed to her laws is assurance of immortality,
> and immortality brings one near to God;
> so the desire for wisdom leads to a kingdom.

This is a *sorites*, a literary form known from Greek literary discussion; in Latin it is referred to as *gradatio* or *climax* and is defined as follows (Fischel 1973: 119):

> The sorites is a set of statements which proceed, step by step, through the force of logic or reliance upon a succession of indisputable facts, to a climactic conclusion, each statement picking up the last key word (or key phrase) of the preceding one.

The author clearly knows of the form and makes effective use of it.

The core of Wisdom 10–19 is a literary form well known from Greek rhetoric known as the *synkrisis* or comparison (Greek *sugkrisis*). This form was used in the *progymnasmata*, the 'preparatory school' phase of education preceding the training directly in rhetoric. The pupils were given exercises using a variety of forms, including the moral anecdote (*chreia*), praise (*encomium*), comparison (*synkrisis*), and the like. The *synkrisis* usually took the form of an antithetical comparison of absolute positions, the one usually being positive and the other negative. A good example of this is the story of Heracles at the crossroads, a moral tale about choosing the good path as opposed to the bad one (Xenophon, *Memorabilia* 2.1.22-33):

> When Heracles was passing from boyhood to youth's estate, wherein the young, now becoming their own masters, show whether they will approach life by the path of virtue or the path of vice, he went out into a quiet place, and sat pondering which road to take. And there appeared two women of great stature making towards him. The one was fair to see and of high bearing; and her limbs were adorned with purity, her eyes with modesty; sober was her figure, and her robe was white. The other was plump and soft, with high feeding. Her face was made up to heighten its natural white and pink, her figure to exaggerate her height. Open-eyed was she; and dressed so as to disclose all her charms.

These women then go on each to present her case to Heracles and contrast the life of virtue with that of vice. This is the sort of comparison to be found widely in Greek literary tradition. Further details on the *synkrisis* are given below in illustrating how the author of the Wisdom of Solomon has combined this Greek form with Jewish tradition to produce a Hellenistic midrash.

The four cardinal virtues (*aretai*) were well known in the Greek sphere, having been commented on already by Plato (*Phaedo* 69C; *Republic* 427E–435A; *Laws* 631C). Wis. 8.7 states,

> And if anyone loves righteousness [*dikaiosunē*],
> her labors are virtues [*aretai*];
> for she teaches self-control [*sōphrosunē*] and prudence [*phronēsis*],
> justice [*dikaiosunē*] and courage [*andreia*];
> nothing in life is more profitable for mortals than these.

The writer lists them here without further discussion, expecting that his readers would immediately identify the reference. His referring to them in a Jewish context indeed creates an incongruity by saying that if one loves *dikaiosunē* ('righteousness'), the fruits include *dikaiosunē*! The writer has used a common word which tends to have the broader connotation of 'righteousness' (even though it can also mean 'justice') in the Jewish tradition in Greek, but the word also happens to be one of the cardinal virtues, where it has the narrower meaning of 'justice'. Hence the slightly jarring repetition of the same word in the immediate context.

Midrash

The term *midrash* (plural *midrashim*) is a Hebrew word meaning 'exposition'. The root of the word *drš* means 'to seek, search, examine', and the earliest reference of the noun *midrash* is apparently to a book (2 Chron. 13.22; 24.27). It is in rabbinic literature that the term takes on the meaning 'scriptural commentary or interpretation'. In modern literary studies the term 'midrash' has been decontextualized from its original Jewish milieu and come to be used to mean interpretation in a broad sense. This usage is rejected here and confined to its meaning in the context of Jewish studies. Much debate has gone on in recent years about the meaning of the term. The best definition in my opinion is the one given by Porton (1981:62; 1992: 819):

> Midrash is a type of literature, oral or written, which has its starting point in a fixed canonical text, considered the revealed word of God by the midrashist and his audience, and in which this original verse is explicitly cited or clearly alluded to.

According to this definition, some passages of the Wisdom of Solomon would seem to embody a type of midrash.

There can be problems when one attempts to apply the term 'midrash' to writings in Greek. The interpretative techniques may be different from those most easily observed in rabbinic literature. The Wisdom of Solomon is written in Greek and has much in its content which is better paralleled from Greek literature than that in Hebrew or Aramaic. Nevertheless, the term 'Hellenistic midrash' has often been used of large sections of Wisdom 10–19. These will now be looked at.

Wisdom 10–19: An Example of a Hellenistic Jewish Midrash

As noted above, it quickly becomes problematic to use the term 'midrash' outside its context in rabbinic literature; however, it is generally accepted that midrash can also be found in some other Jewish writings, including the Septuagint, the Qumran *pesharim* (commentaries), and 'rewritten Bible' works such as *Jubilees* and Pseudo-Philo (*Liber Antiquitatum Biblicarum*). A large section of the Wisdom of Solomon Book of History is devoted to drawing on biblical examples from Genesis and Exodus to make the writer's point and get across his message about his own contemporary situation (see Schwenk-Bressler 1993). The term 'Hellenistic Jewish midrash' seems to be appropriate in this particular instance. That is, it makes use of biblical examples evidently taken from the canonical text (and thus serving as an implicit textual citation) and draws on the known Jewish tradition. On the other hand, there is much in the context which has been derived from Greek literature and rhetoric.

There are actually two midrashim in Wisdom 10–19, though the one runs without a clear break into the second. The formal structure of the two is different, however. The first covers only ch. 10 and follows the fortunes of biblical history to the time of Moses. The subject is wisdom, and it is wisdom's activity in guiding mankind—especially the chosen people—which is the point of the survey of history found here. She guarded the 'first-formed father' Adam and delivered him from his sin (10.1). Note that while Adam's sin is acknowledged, the author does not dwell on it, perhaps because to do so might detract from the positive picture of wisdom given. He does not seem to have suffered from the curse pronounced in Genesis 3. An unrighteous man (Cain) perished in his rage and caused the earth to be drowned. This ascription of the flood of Noah to Cain seems to be a unique tradition. The immediate cause in Gen. 6.1-4 seems to be the sin of the 'sons of God', though the precise meaning of this passage is unclear. In 1 Enoch 6–9 the cause of the flood is the sin of the fallen angels with human women, their giant offspring who destroy the earth, and the evil spirits who arise from the death of the giants.

As already noted, the emphasis is on the activity of wisdom, and the individuals named are not all 'heroes' (e.g., Cain). Nevertheless, there is some affinity with the lists of the 'great men of Israel', the prime example of which is the list in Ben Sira 44–50 (cf. Mack 1985). They seem to be presented anonymously for a particular reason, however. They are meant to be taken as models or types rather than just to be admired as heroes. They are the righteous and serve as a bridge between the righteous individual in the earlier chapters of the book and the righteous people of Israel in the later chapters (Reese 1970: 119, 144-45).

Although the midrash on the plagues of Exodus 7–12 (11.1-14; 16.1–19.22) follows seamlessly from the survey of history in Wisdom 10, it has a different literary form and can for this reason be considered a separate midrash. It is in the form of a *synkrisis*, a set of antitheses contrasting the sufferings of the Egyptians in the plagues and the parallels (see pp. 37-38 above). It shows how the Bible could be interpreted in a Hellenistic context, how a midrash can be found outside rabbinic literature. It is important to make this point because some still wish to see a close connection between this section of the Wisdom of Solomon and rabbinic literature. A good example is the classic article of Edmund Stein (1934), who collected a number of parallels to these chapters from rabbinic literature. While these parallels have their own interest, what he failed to show is that they demonstrate dependence of the author on Semitic or Palestinian or rabbinic sources (cf. Heinemann 1948). It has regularly been proposed that Hellenistic writers such as the author of the Wisdom of Solomon and Philo have depended on the rabbis or 'old Palestinian allegory' or something similar. Each writing must be examined separately, of course, since some Jewish Greek writings may indeed have had a Semitic source, but it must be kept in mind that rabbinic writings are from much later in their present form, and critical scholars are now much more hesitant about retrojecting later rabbinic statements into a much earlier period without very careful argument. In the case of Philo, the proposed arguments have not been convincing (Heinemann 1932; Grabbe 1988: 66-77; Grabbe 1991).

Although examples of antitheses such as occur in Wisdom 11-19 can probably be found in a wide variety of religious literature, it was a form highly developed in the Greco–Roman literary context. Thus the form is Hellenistic but the content is based on Jewish tradition; on the other hand, the tradition has been adapted and interpreted into something new, some of it by means of a Hellenistic eye quite outside the perspective of the Old Testament writers. There are ten plagues in the book of Exodus, but the writer draws on only part of them. Grimm already pointed out three principles used in constructing the antitheses here (1837: 331; cf. van Rooden 1986: 82-83):

(1) The Israelites benefit by the very things which serve to punish their enemies (11.5): 'For through the very things by which their enemies were punished, they themselves received benefit in their need.'

(2) The *lex talionis* or principle of punishment by the means of the sin (11.16): 'one is punished by the very things by which one sins.'

(3) Israel itself should suffer a mild form of the punishments of her enemies, so that she might understand the mercies of God (cf. 16.4).

The realization of these principles can be illustrated in graphic form by a chart (cf. Stein 1934: 574 n. 2; Heinemann 1948: 242; Gilbert 1986: 87):

Sin	Plague	Benefits
I Killing of infants in Nile (11.7)	1 Waters of Nile undrinkable	Water from the rock in the desert
II Animals worshiped (11.15)	2 Animals (frogs) ruin appetites	Quail provided miraculously
	3 Animals which kill	Saved from serpents
III Refusal to recognize God (16.16)	4 Destruction of foodstuffs by fire/hail	Manna from heaven
IV Captivity of Israelites (18.4)	5 Captive by darkness	Column of fire
V Killing of infants in Nile (18.5)	6 Death of the firstborn	Aaron stops the plague?
	7 Egyptians drowned in Red Sea	Israelites pass through the Red Sea

Five sins are committed, though the last is a repeat of the first. There are seven antitheses in which the Egyptians suffer and the Israelites benefit. As will be clear, these do not follow through consistently the three principles listed above. Perhaps we should not expect the third principle (that the Israelites also suffered) to be carried through with all the incidents, but we might expect it with the first and second principles. For example, in plague 3 Israel does not benefit from the instrument of the Egyptian suffering; they are simply saved from an analogous animal plague. But perhaps this is asking the writer to be too consistent, and there is a rough correlation.

An important aspect of the writer's interpretation is its sanitizing of the story. In Exodus and Numbers, the Israelites are very human, quickly losing their determination and raising complaints when things go badly. None of this appears in the story here. Instead of a very human group, they have become a sinless community of saints (van Rooden 1986: 88). Nothing negative is said about their behavior. Even the rebellion of Korah, Dathan, and Abiram which brought on a plague against Israel is treated so circumspectly that only the suffering of the Israelites is mentioned but no hint that it was the result of sin (Wis. 18.20). There is no development or growth because they have evidently already reached perfection. One thinks also of other Hellenistic writers on Jewish history, such as Josephus (who, for example, omits the incident of the golden calf from his account).

Cosmology is important to the Wisdom of Solomon, as will be discussed later (pp. 64-66). For purposes of the midrash here, there is evidence that the writer has partially constructed his narrative around Greco–Roman views about the physical world (van Rooden 1986). Here the cosmos cooperates to assist the Israelites (16.24), an idea already known from the Old Testament (e.g., Josh. 10.11-14; Judg. 5.20). Nature is turned upside down so that land animals become sea animals and vice versa (19.19), which probably has reference to such incidents as the quail coming from the sea and even the people's passing through the Red Sea (or not, in the case of the Egyptians). But the elements are also said to have changed their order (19.18). There was a view that each element was associated with the habitat of particular animals (Plato, *Timaeus* 39E; Cicero, *De Natura Deorum* 2.42). The Wisdom of Solomon has apparently developed a scheme in which each of the four elements of classical antiquity is associated with one of the antitheses:

Water: frogs come from the river; quail, from the sea (Second Antithesis: 16.1-4)
Earth: locusts and flies come from the ground (Third Antithesis: 16.5-14)
Fire: fire from heaven (Fourth Antithesis: 16.15-29)
Air: darkness caused by strange atmosphere (Fifth Antithesis: 17.1–18.4)

The plague of darkness might seem odd to associate with air. The Greek for air is *aēr*, however, and originally meant a mist or fog. Although it came to mean 'air' in the sense of atmosphere, the original meaning was not lost. It was also symbolic of death and the netherworld, the very terrors suffered by the Egyptians during this plague (van Rooden 1986: 90-92).

Another passage hinted at by the Wisdom of Solomon in this section seems to be Exodus 15 (Gilbert 1984: 305-306). The key is the allusion to Exodus 15 at 10.20-21 and 19.9. There is also an emphasis on water in the context of the two key verses. Thus, we apparently find another concentric structure as in other sections (pp. 18-23), except that the central element has a parallel at the end:

A Allusions to Exodus15   10.20
  B Plague of water   11.1-14
    C Pharaoh's decree   11.6
      D Role of creation   16.24-25
    C' Pharaoh's decree   18.5
  B´ Plague of water   19.1-9
A´ Allusion to Exodus 15   19.9
      D' Role of creation   19.10-12, 18-21

If this analysis is correct, the section of antitheses (but minus the digressions) is marked off by an *inclusio* (p. 19) and thus further indicated to be a unity.

Other Possible Midrashim

Other portions of the book can be considered biblical interpretation
and thus possible examples of midrash. Chapters 6–9 have Solomon as
their subject. Here is an interpreted Solomon. It is not clear how seri-
ously the author wished to have his 'Solomon' taken as authentic, but
the Solomon he presents is not the same as that known from the Hebrew canon. Much of this section is not focused on Solomon directly but
on wisdom and his quest for her, so the additions to the biblical
account tend to seem trivial, such as having a good soul assigned to him
(8.19-20). But what comes across from this spattering of details is a
Hellenistic Solomon. His quest for wisdom, his gaining her by prayer,
preferring her to wealth, and the like are known from the Old
Testament tradition. Nevertheless, Solomon here is a figure at home in
the Greek world. He is presented as both the ideal king and the ideal
sage. Naturally, these images draw on the Israelite wisdom tradition, but
there is also evidence that much has fed in from the Hellenistic side.
See further on kingship at pp. 63-64.

Wisdom 1–6 is another section rich in midrashic activity, if a number
of recent studies have any validity. J. Schaberg (1982) has briefly noted
that Psalm 2 underlies a number of passages in the Book of Eschatology:

> Ps. 2.1-3//Wis. 2.10-20: wicked conspire against God and the righteous.
> Ps. 2.2//Wis. 1.1: address to rulers of the earth.
> Ps. 2.4//Wis. 4.8: God will laugh them to scorn.
> Ps. 2.7//Wis. 2.18: God's son.
> Ps. 2.9//Wis. 4.19: God will break them.
> Ps. 2.10//Wis. 6.1: learn and understand, O rulers.
> Ps. 2.11//Wis. 6.21: admonition (to serve Yahweh/honor wisdom).

Another possible midrash may be found in Wis. 2.10–5.23. M.J.
Suggs (1957) has argued that it is based on the Fourth Servant Song in
Isa. 52.13–53.12 (though he was not the first to make the connection;
see Nickelsburg 1972: 61 n. 47). He points to the following parallels
that provide evidence of an interpretation built around the term *pais*
('child') in the Septuagint of Isa. 52.2, 13:

> Wis. 2.13-16 makes reference to *pais*.
> Wis. 2.19-20//Isa. 53.7-9.
> Wis. 3.2-3//Isa. 53.4.
> Wis. 3.6//Isa. 53.7-10.
> Wis. 4.19//Isa. 52.15.
> Wis. 5.2//Isa.52.14.

Wis. 5.3-4//Isa. 53.3, 10.
Wis. 5.6//Isa. 53.6.

Suggs (1957) also notes parallel passages for this section of the Wisdom of Solomon from elsewhere in Isaiah to supplement those from the Fourth Servant Song. According to him, the experiences of the *huios* ('son') of the Wisdom of Solomon are the same as those of the *pais* in Isaiah, even if there is very little verbal correspondence.

George Nickelsburg (1972: 62-66) points to close counterparts between Wis. 5.1-8 and Isa. 52.13–53.6 which are also paralleled by 1 Enoch 62–63:

Common Event	Isaiah	Wisdom	1 Enoch
A God speaks	52.13	—	62.1
B Exaltation	52.13	5.1	62.2a
C Audience	52.15	5.1	62.3ab
D They see the Exalted One	52.15	5.2	62.3c
E Their reaction	52.15	5.2	62.4-5
F Recognition	implied	5.4	62.1b, 3c
G Confession of sins	53.1-6	5.4-8	63.1-11
H Acclamation by audience	53.4-6	5.5	62.6, 9
			63.2-3

His argument is not that the Wisdom of Solomon has borrowed from 1 Enoch but that both 1 Enoch and the Wisdom of Solomon have drawn on a common tradition in Isaiah 52–53—and what they have in common is not just the biblical text. On the contrary, the Isaian servant tradition has already been interpreted in the light of the Son of Man tradition (known to us primarily from Daniel 7). Nickelsburg's main point is that Wisdom 2 and 4–5 conform to the common structural pattern of the persecution and exaltation of the righteous. He has argued that this pattern is common to a variety of wisdom tales, including the Joseph story, Ahiqar, Esther, Daniel 3 and 6, Susanna, 2 Maccabees 7, and 3 Maccabees.

Jane Schaberg has built on this, taking the Isaiah and Psalms backgrounds for granted but looking for further Old Testament texts underlying Wisdom 1–6. She makes a convincing case that Daniel was used by the author of the Wisdom of Solomon in a number of passages. More problematic is her contention that the persecuted righteous person of Wisdom 1–6 is based primarily on the figure of Enoch. Enoch does indeed seem to be alluded to in Wis. 4.10, but there is no need to assume that the description of the righteous is confined to Enoch. Especially significant is Enoch's lack of mention in Wis. 10.3-4—rather surprising if Enoch was the model of the righteous man.

Just as Nickelsburg saw the model of the persecution and exaltation of the righteous enacted in Wisdom 2 and 4–5, M. Kolarcik (1991: 63-131) has recently developed the thesis that Wis. 2–5 takes the form of a trial scene (cf. Nickelsburg 1972: 88-89). But it is no ordinary trial scene since it shades into apocalyptic judgment. Kolarcik's position is based in part on the structure of Wisdom 1–6. The verbal attack of the wicked on the righteous quickly takes on the shape of a defence. They accuse the righteous person, but then the positions are inverted and they are (silently) accused by the righteous and must defend themselves. They mount their defence by attacking the righteous and even plan the ultimate accusation: plotting his death. Their refutation is the blessedness of the righteous in the afterlife, which forces the wicked to confess their guilt. It all ends in a final judgment on God's enemies (Wis. 5.15-23; see also pp. 55-57).

The use of the trial scenario has several advantages (Kolarcik 1991: 185): it can accommodate the dramatic issues of life and death; it allows different perspectives to be explored and also 'exposed'; it allows the interpretation of events in the light of the 'ambiguity of death', a topic of considerable importance to the writer (see pp. 52-53). A particular aim of the writer, which the trial imagery serves well, is to show the origins of the wrong thinking engaged in by the wicked, primarily their view of death (see pp. 50-51). The final address to the rulers in Wisdom 6 serves as the exhortation to understand the meaning of the trial scene. The Book of Wisdom follows, presenting wisdom as the means to justice and God. The Book of History reinforces the message by showing that interaction between Israel and the Egyptians in history was a prefiguring of the relations between the righteous and wicked discussed in Wisdom 1–6. Thus, Kolarcik sees the trial imagery as a key to understanding the message of the book.

Further Reading

On Hellenization and the Jews, with discussion of the major positions and bibliography, see Grabbe (1992), especially ch. 2.

On the supposed contrast of Greek thought and Hebrew thought, see Barr (1961; 1966).

A good account of the Biblical Theology Movement, which fostered the 'Hebrew versus Greek thought' concept, is given by Childs (1970).

For the fragmentary Jewish writers in Greek, who are so important for our understanding of biblical interpretation in 'Hellenistic Judaism', see the convenient edition and commentaries by Holladay (1983; 1989; 1995).

On the text of the Wisdom of Solomon, the question of its original language, and its unity, see especially Gilbert (1984; 1986: 58-65, 87-91); Larcher (1983–85: I, 53-119); Schürer (1986: III, 568-79); Zimmerman (1966–67: 1-27, 101-35).

The most extensive study of allegory in classical antiquity is Pépin (1976).

For a study of one aspect of Philo's allegorical exegesis, namely, his etymologizing of Hebrew names, see Grabbe (1988).

The main study of the Hellenistic material in the Wisdom of Solomon remains Reese (1970).

Other studies useful for the Hellenistic background of the Wisdom of Solomon include Fischel (1973: 119-51).

A study of one form of the *progymnasmata*, with an introduction to the subject, can be found in Hock and O'Neil (1986).

On the definition of 'midrash', see Porton (1981: 55-92; 1992: IV, 818-22).

On the question of rabbinic sources for the Wisdom of Solomon and some other Jewish Hellenistic writers such as Philo, see Grabbe (1988: 66-77; 1991: 153-66); Heinemann (1932/1962; 1948: 241-51); Stein (1934: 558-75).

Apart from those just listed, some of the other studies relating midrash to the Wisdom of Solomon are the following: Nickelsburg (1972: 49-92); van Rooden (1986: 81-96); Schaberg (1982: 75-101); Schwenk-Bressler (1993); Suggs (1957: 26-33).

On the 'heroes' of Ben Sira 44–50, see Mack (1985).

3

THE MESSAGE OF THE BOOK

Introduction

The Book of Wisdom covers a number of theological themes and topics. Its precise audience can be debated (see pp. 91-92), but much can be said about the message of the book without having to be specific about the recipients. In discussing the unity of the book, some scholars have pointed to several themes running through the book. For example, Reese (1970: 140-45) notes five such themes:

(1) Religious knowledge of God;
(2) Theological use of the concept of 'seeing';
(3) Interaction of malice and ignorance;
(4) Human immortality and related themes;
(5) Didactic use of history.

Most of these are discussed in some form or other below. However, it should be noted that a theme is not nessarily the same as a theological topic. For example, the use of the imagery of 'seeing' is an important compositional device of the writer, but it does not seem to be central to the writer's *message*. Similarly, the didactic use of history is a *means* rather than an end.

In this chapter an attempt will be made to deal with some of the main issues in the Wisdom of Solomon. The important figure of wisdom is not treated here but has its own chapter (ch. 4).

The Righteous and the Wicked

The book begins in the first chapter with a picture of the righteous and the wicked—as if the author wanted to make it immediately clear that this was a major concern. The theme of righteousness and wickedness and the contrast between them and their fates continues through the book.

The wicked are going to be punished (3.10-11); so much could be taken for granted. More surprisingly, the assumption is made that wickedness is a family affair (3.12). The wives of the wicked are mindless; their children are also wicked; their whole generation is under a curse. The children of adulterers will not grow up (3.16). Having offspring and descendants was considered extremely important in the Jewish tradition; and dying without descendants, the worst of calamities. Yet, for some reason, the writer seems to assume that the wicked have children; it is the righteous who are thought to be childless in some instances (3.13-15; 4.1-9). This is a theme similar to that in Isaiah 58 in which the law-abiding eunuch would receive a reward greater than children. Thus, the author tacitly recognizes that things do not always go well with the righteous, but he assumes that it will be resolved in the end.

The assumed short life of the wicked, taken to be part of their punishment, may be matched by a similar short span of years for the righteous (4.7); however, in this case the apparent misfortune is only illusory. In fact, the early death of the righteous is a blessing because they have been removed before they can be corrupted by wickedness (4.11). Span of life, maturity of years, and the seniority of old age are not measured by chronological time but by lifestyle and mode of living (4.8-9). One is an 'elder' by reason of righteous behavior rather than because of age.

In many ways, this picture of the wicked and righteous is a simplistic one. In the Israelite traditions the problem of suffering came to be recognized as a singular problem in a theology which assumed a righteous, sovereign God. Some strands of the tradition (e.g., Deuteronomy) did indeed assume a deed–consequence relationship—that righteousness would be rewarded and wickedness punished, because this was a part of the divine order. But others saw that things were not so simple. The book of Job, one of the world's great pieces of literature, explored at length the problem of theodicy. The book of Qohelet or Ecclesiastes addresses in its own way a similar problem, if from a different perspective. Theologians in both the Jewish and Christian traditions have been wrestling with the challenge ever since, even if they have not always understood the two great wisdom books.

The writers of Job and Qohelet were geniuses born out of their time, and later literature did not generally understand their sophisticated

approach, electing instead to revert to simple black-and-white moral
tales (cf. the *Testament of Job* with the book of Job). The Wisdom of
Solomon follows this pattern and returns to the naive view that the
wicked will not enjoy the fruits of their wickedness. The writer goes so
far as to suggest that there is not even short-term enjoyment (4.3-6);
they certainly do not benefit if they live a long time (3.16-19; 4.16;
5.8-14). Of course, one reason the perspective of the Wisdom of
Solomon is so different from that of Job and Qoholet is that the former
presupposes an afterlife whereas the latter two do not. One can always
solve the problems of this world by appeal to the unseen next one!

Interestingly, the attitude alleged to be that of the wicked is very
much that espoused by many ordinary people today (2.1-6):

> For they reasoned unsoundly, saying to themselves,
> 'Short and sorrowful is our life,
> and there is no remedy when a life comes to its end,
> and no one has been known to return from Hades.
> For we were born by mere chance,
> and hereafter we shall be as though we had never been,
> for the breath in our nostrils is smoke,
> and reason is a spark kindled by the beating of our hearts;
> when it is extinguished, the body will turn to ashes,
> and the spirit will dissolve like empty air.
> Our name will be forgotten in time,
> and no one will remember our works;
> our life will pass away like the traces of a cloud,
> and be scattered like mist
> that is chased by the rays of the sun
> and overcome by its heat.
> For our allotted time is the passing of a shadow,
> and there is no return from our death,
> because it is sealed up and no one turns back.'
> Come, therefore, let us enjoy the good things that exist,
> and make use of the creation to the full as in youth.

Or to put it more prosaically, 'Eat, drink, and be merry, for tomorrow
we die!' (Isa. 22.13). Although this view is common in our secular age,
it was very much a minority view in the Roman empire. A genuine
atheist was a rare individual, though one occasionally sees comments
such as the following which dismisses Roman mythology about the
underworld *(Epigrammata Graeca* #646, translation from Lattimore
1962: 75):

> There is no boat in Hades, no ferry man Charon, no Aeacus keeper of the
> keys, nor any dog called Cerberus. All of us who have died and gone below
> are bones and ashes: there is nothing else.

On the other hand, some individuals were accused of being atheists, especially the Epicureans. Epicurus (c. 341–c. 270 BCE) developed a philosophy based on the scientific theory credited to Democritus and Leucippus, the atomic theory. The argument was that all things were made of atoms and void (space), and that the world and all living things arose by an accidental conglomeration of atoms. The gods were assumed to exist and to live eternally (because made of especially fine atoms) and to be worthy of worship. On the other hand, they were not believed to have anything to do with either the origin or the maintenance of the world. Thus, the Epicureans could be said to be practical atheists even though they believed in the gods.

The lifestyle espoused by Epicurus was that of simplicity and moderation; nevertheless, it was often caricatured as one of excess, indulgence, and even lascivity. There is no evidence that the writer of the Wisdom of Solomon had the Epicureans specifically in mind—indeed, it is unlikely they were the main target of the author, but it is their system which fits most closely the views expressed here. Perhaps the writer considers them representative of the attitudes being condemned. (If so, it is a gross caricature, since the Epicureans did not espouse a life without virtue or morality.) But the Wisdom of Solomon goes on to speak more negatively than just about living for the present (2.10-20): the wicked desire to oppress the righteous, the poor, the elderly, and other vulnerable people. The reason given is slightly suspect. The wicked attack the righteous because they reproach them for their sins. Even more than this, the assumption seems to be that the wicked have an irrational antipathy for the righteous; the very existence of the righteous is an affront to the wicked. So the wicked attack the righteous to see whether God will deliver them.

The righteous are never directly identified with the Jews, nor the wicked with the Gentiles. Since righteousness is closely associated with obedience to the law and knowledge of God (2.12), one would expect the righteous to be confined mostly to the Jewish people, but whether the author might have conceived of a 'righteous Gentile' is difficult to know. Similarly, to what extent the company of wicked was thought to include Jews is unclear, though no doubt apostates (however defined) would have been included. The Wisdom of Solomon prefers to deal in generic types rather than specific identified groups.

'The Ambiguity of Death'

The meaning and significance of the writer's use of death as a term has occasioned a good deal of discussion over the years, in part because there is an 'ambiguity' in the use of the expression. A monograph has recently been devoted to the topic (Kolarcik 1991). As described in greater detail on p. 46, Kolarcik has argued that the writer makes use of trial imagery in Wisdom 2–5 because this is a way of exploring the 'ambiguity of death' and furthering his message about justice.

According to Kolarcik, death is used in three different senses in the book: (a) mortality, (b) physical death as punishment, and (c) ultimate death (156-58), defined as separation from God and the cosmos (170). Surprisingly, general human mortality is not considered a consequence of sin; that is, there is no suggestion in the book that the sin of Adam brought mortality to human beings (Kolarcik 1991: 146). By 'ambiguity' is not meant that the writer himself was uncertain but rather the fact that at the surface level of the text, the distinction between the three senses is often left unspecified. The purpose of this is that it allows the subject to be explored from all angles, that of the wicked as well as of the righteous.

The writer has two aims: negatively, to refute the false notion of death held by the wicked and, positively, to persuade the reader to love justice and God (Kolarcik 1991: 160). The view of death by the wicked is a self-fulfilling prophecy: because of their view of death, brought about by their false reasoning and injustice, they experience the very extinction in which they believed in the first place. In that sense their physical death is a punishment, whereas the physical death of the righteous is only a passage to the blissful afterlife. In the last two parts of book, the righteous and wicked individuals become represented by the communities of Israel and the Egyptians: 'The interpretation of the plagues and the crossing of the sea is presented in apocalyptic fashion with the imagery of the changing of the elements' (Kolarcik 1991: 176; cf. pp. 42-43). The two views and interpretations of death remain the same, however. The conclusions can be summarized as follows (Kolarcik 1991: 168-70):

> In the specific argumentation of the author, mortality is seen from two opposing perspectives, from that of the wicked and from that of the just. Mortality as such remains inherently ambiguous; it is open to different assessments. For the author, it is a condition from which the just realize their union with God through a virtuous life; for the wicked it is a condition which signifies ultimate meaninglessness.

The mortality of the just is viewed positively in relation to God as a final moment of self-surrender to the divine. In their false reasoning, mortality is judged by the wicked to be the ultimate, destructive fate of human destiny from which no value can be derived. The ironic twist in the wicked's reasoning, as the author presents it, is that by their own decisions they bring on the very fate which they so much despise and mask. By despising weakness and mortality, the wicked receive the sentence of an ultimate death which is far more tragic than even their original ruminations on their fate suggest.

Knowledge and Ignorance

Knowledge is an important subject to the author. Knowledge has salvific value; knowledge of God is the key to immortality (2.13; 15.3). Conversely, the wicked do not know God (5.7; 3.10-11; 13.1-3; cf. 2.13; 15.1-3). The key to knowledge is the figure of wisdom. She is the source of knowledge of all sorts.

This emphasis on knowledge helps to explain the model of 'Solomon' in Wisdom 6–10. Here Solomon is presented as the ideal sage, among other things (Lohse 1971: 459-63). He is not just the pious Jew concerned with faithfulness to his religion and the law of God (though both these are assumed). More than this, his quest for wisdom in these chapters is to gain knowledge and understanding. This knowledge includes moral values and virtues (7.22-24), but it also includes esoteric knowledge about the mysteries of nature, cosmology, the past and future (7.16-22; 8.8-16). These are the traditional pursuits of the sage in the Israelite wisdom tradition, but they also represent the areas of interest to the Hellenistic sage (see further on pp. 63-64).

Immortality and the Soul

It has often been asserted in modern theology that the resurrection of the dead is the characteristic Jewish form of eschatology, whereas the immortality of the soul is Greek. The Wisdom of Solomon would hardly recognize this distinction! The origin of both the immortality of the soul and the resurrection of the dead in Judaism are the subject of debate, but the concept of the soul which survives the death of the individual appears as early as the concept of the resurrection, as far as extant Jewish literature is concerned. The idea of the immortal soul may well have been borrowed from the Greeks; on the other hand, the resurrection may have been borrowed from the Persians. The distinction made has no historical justification.

In early Greek literature, the picture of death and Hades found in Homer is similar to that presupposed in much of the Old Testament literature. That is, something leaves the body at death and survives in shadowy form in the underworld (the realm of Hades in Homer; Sheol in the Old Testament). But this shade or soul or *nephesh* is not the person; the person as such disintegrated at death. To what extent the literary construct represents the views of ordinary people is always a question. Although scholars are generally agreed that the early Old Testament books envisage no afterlife, it has been argued that Israelites as a whole held a somewhat different view or views. The cult of the dead was certainly practiced, though this has different meaning to different communities. Some think a 'beatific afterlife' was believed in by many Israelites at a time when the 'official' transmitters of the literature opposed the view (cf. Grabbe 1995b: 141-45, and the literature discussed there).

Among the Greeks, we know that the worldview of Homer and Hesiod (eighth century BCE?) was not maintained (assuming it ever represented the general view among the people). Some centuries later the Pythagoreans and Orphics held the view that the soul was essentially the person. The slogan *sōma sēma* 'body/tomb' was even coined to express the idea that the body was the prison or tomb of the soul, and the soul (as the person) had the goal of attempting to free itself from being weighted down by the body. This became the basic position in Platonism. The position in Stoicism was somewhat more complicated, though it had many points in common with Platonism, while the Epicurean view rejected any afterlife.

It was a view of the soul similar to that in Platonism which became widespread in Judaism in the last century or so BCE. According to Josephus, both the Pharisees and Essenes held beliefs which assumed the immortality of the soul; however, the Sadducees rejected such views and clung to the earlier position of no afterlife attested in much of the Old Testament (*War* 2.8.14 §§162-65; *Ant.* 18.1.3 §§14). The Pharisees also believed in the resurrection, though whether the Essenes did as well is debated. Therefore, the question of the ultimate origin is irrelevant since both the idea of the resurrection and the concept of the soul became intimate parts of Judaism. Neither is 'more characteristic' of Judaism than the other, and some sections of Judaism continued to reject one or the other, or both.

The subject of immortality and future existence is intimately tied up with the subject of the righteous and the wicked. Already in 1.13-15 it is stated that God did not create death and does not delight in it; on the contrary, he created life, and righteousness is itself immortal. The goal of life is immortality, and the soul at least has the potential for immortality in it (2.23; 3.4). Less clear is whether the soul is naturally immortal. The precise view of the Wisdom of Solomon on the soul is not immediately clear. The text seems to suggest that immortality was a gift to the righteous, not an inherent condition of the soul itself (3.4; 4.1; 8.13, 17; 15.3). It has been suggested that the Wisdom of Solomon expresses an Aristotelean viewpoint rather than a Platonic (Reese 1970: 80-82); in other words the soul and body are not independent substances. Whether this is true is a matter of debate, but it illustrates the difficulty in trying to understand the position of the writer.

The author of the Wisdom of Solomon also held to a doctrine which was not a necessary accompaniment to belief in an immortal soul. In 8.19-20, 'Solomon' claims,

> As a child I was naturally gifted,
> and a good soul fell to my lot;
> or rather, being good, I entered an undefiled body.

This could imply *metempsychosis*, or the transmigration of souls (also said to be a belief of the Pharisees by Josephus, *War* 2.8.14 §163). It would assume that Solomon's soul was good because of effort in a previous life. However, this is not explicitly stated, and it may just be that his soul was created by God to enter the body being prepared for him at the time of birth. This raises all sorts of questions about why he inherited a good soul, how he was chosen for the privilege, whether souls were predestined to be good or bad, and so on. Unfortunately, the author does not answer many of the questions he raises.

Apocalypticism and the Reward of the Righteous and Wicked

The reward of the righteous and wicked is not spelled out in detail, but there are some general indications in Wisdom 3 and 5. Kolarcik has noted the similarities between the descriptions and apocalyptic language (1991: 106-107). Before looking at these passages in detail, it would be useful to say something about apocalypticism. Although a good deal of scholarly discussion about the genre of apocalypse has taken place in recent years, there is still no fully agreed definition. The phenomenon of apocalypticism is even more difficult to define. Some would argue that apocalypticism is foreign to books such as the Wisdom of Solomon,

which is certainly no apocalypse, but the question is whether non-apoc-
alypses can exhibit apocalypticism.

Apocalypticism (some prefer 'apocalyptic') is generally thought to be
characterized by 'apocalyptic eschatology'. This may include an end of
the world in catastrophic circumstances, with a resurrection, final judgment, and new heavens and a new earth. But this is not the only form
it might take. Some have argued that transcendence of death is at the
base of apocalyptic eschatology (cf. Collins 1974). In other words, personal survival by means of an immortal soul is as much a sign of apocalypticism as cosmic cataclysm and the like.

The reward of the righteous is clearly presented in Wisdom 3–5 as including immortality and an eternal afterlife. Some verses go beyond this.
According to 3.7-9,

> In the time of their visitation they will shine forth,
> and will run like sparks through the stubble.
> They will govern nations and rule over peoples,
> and the Lord will reign over them forever.
> Those who trust in him will understand truth,
> and the faithful will abide with him in love,
> because grace and mercy are upon his holy ones,
> and he watches over his elect.

This seems to presuppose what has sometimes been referred to as 'astral
immortality' (Dupont-Sommer 1949). This is the view that the righteous became like the stars of heaven at death. The concept is evidently
first attested in Dan. 12.3: 'Those who are wise shall shine like the
brightness of the sky,…like the stars forever.' This could imply that they
became angels since stars were often thought of as angels (cf. Collins
1974; Charlesworth 1980).

The righteous are numbered among the children of God and their
lot is among the saints (5.5). Among their duties will be to rule with
God, being crowned with a glorious crown (5.15-16). This rule would
apparently include judging the wicked, as is described in 5.15-23:

> The Lord will take his zeal as his whole armor,
> and will arm all creation to repel his enemies;
> …
> and creation will join with him to fight against his frenzied foes.
> Shafts of lightning will fly with true aim,
> and will leap from the clouds to the target, as from a well-drawn bow,
> and hailstones full of wrath will be hurled as from a catapult;
> the water of the sea will rage against them,
> and rivers will relentlessly overwhelm them;
> a mighty wind will rise against them,

and like a tempest it will winnow them away.
Lawlessness will lay waste the whole earth,
and evil-doing will overturn the thrones of rulers.

This description of a judgment on God's enemies—the wicked—in which he fights like a heavenly warrior and enlists the very cosmos in his battle makes strong use of apocalyptic imagery. God has strapped on his armor (5.17-20) and gone out to fight his foes. Although this is a part of the judgment on them in this life, it does not preclude a later, post-mortem judgment as well. Unfortunately, the Wisdom of Solomon does not go into detail about such a judgment.

Idol Worship and Polytheism

The Wisdom of Solomon is vehement about idol worship. As in other Jewish literature of the time, the use of images in worship is viewed with horror and disgust. Harangues against idols make up a significant part of the third part of the book, especially 12.24–13.19. This includes not only worship of physical objects but also worship of animals and of nature. The author sees a threefold progression of disgust and blame: nature worship (13.1-9: by the more philosophical), idol worship (13.10–15.17), worship of animals (15.18-19: by the Egyptians, the lowest of the low).

The Wisdom of Solomon's arguments are not new. A similar approach is already found in Jer. 10.1-16 and Isa. 44.9-20. Idols are inanimate objects. They have to be nailed down so they do not fall over. A man takes a piece of wood, burns part of it for warmth and heat to cook his food, and makes the rest into an image. Such different uses of the same mundane material are considered a blatant contradiction and deserving of scathing sarcasm. Similar attacks occur in the Epistle of Jeremiah (= 1 Baruch 6). The Wisdom of Solomon uses much the same argument (13.11-19): the woodcutter selects a tree and first produces a vessel for everyday use, with the leavings of his woodwork used to make a fire to heat his meal. The useless knotty part of the wood remaining is then turned into an image, fastened to the wall, and prayed to about the most intimate things in the man's life. A dead thing is prayed to for life; health is sought from the weak; advice on making a journey is derived from the immobile; the voyager calls for protection upon a piece of wood less substantial than the ship on which he sails.

Another image is used a bit later, that of the potter (15.7-13). Here the condemnation is stronger and more bitter. The same imagery is used, that the vessels for common, even lowly use, are made from the same substance as the divine image. Whereas the woodcarver is allowed to produce a work of art (14.19-20), the potter makes the idol from clay—from which we all came and to which we shall all return. In so doing, he has a heart of ashes and a hope cheaper than dirt. The entire reason for doing so is of the basest sort; it is solely for the pupose of making money (15.12). They know that they sin!—or so the Wisdom of Solomon states.

As so often with polemic, the writer has made no attempt to understand or be fair to those who use images. If he had, he would not have accused polytheists of assuming the object of wood or metal was the god itself; rather, it only represented the god. It is true that the connection between the god and the image was often established by a formal ceremony. For example, in Egypt the 'Opening of the Mouth' ceremony was performed for each new divine image. A similar ritual was conducted in Mesopotamia. Even though the god was omnipresent, there was a special way in which the divine presence could be found in the particular statues in question. Nevertheless, the argument of the Wisdom of Solomon and other Jewish writings is simplistic and distorted, making no effort to understand the other religion, and certainly not an analysis to be emulated today by proponents of aniconic worship. The worshiper would have defended the use of images much as those who use statues, icons, and the crucifix in much Christian worship today. For example, Plato writes (*Laws* 931A):

> The ancient laws of all men concerning the gods are two-fold: some of the gods whom we honour we see clearly, but of others we set up statues as images, and we believe that when we worship these, lifeless though they be, the living gods beyond feel great good-will towards us and gratitude.

A similiar statement is found in Plotinus (4.3.11).

Yet the Jewish attack on images was not without parallel in Greco–Roman writings (as quoted by Clement of Alexandria 2.24):

> And another, taking an image of Hercules made of wood (for he happened most likely to be cooking something at home), said, 'Come now, Hercules; now is the time to undergo for us this thirteenth labour, as you did the twelve for Eurystheus, and make this ready for Diagoras,' and so cast it into the fire as a log of wood.

Horace writes in similar vein about a statue of Priapus (*Satires* 1.8.1-7):

> Once I was a fig-wood stem, a worthless log, when the carpenter, doubtful whether to make a stool or a Priapus, chose that I be a god. A god, then, I became, of thieves and birds the special terror; for thieves my right hand

> keeps in check, and this red stake, protruding from unsightly groin; while for
> the mischievous birds, a reed set on my head affrights them and keeps them
> from lighting in the new park.

For the author of the Wisdom of Solomon, idol worship and polytheism are the cause of every evil (14.12, 27):

> For the idea of making idols was the beginning of fornication, and the inven-
> tion of them was the corruption of life...For the worship of idols not to be
> named is the beginning and cause and end of every evil.

Every sort of corruption and sin is traced to using material objects in
worship: child murder, secret rites, pollution of marriages, adultery,
bloodshed, murder, theft, deceit, sexual perversion, and debauchery.
They do not expect to be punished for false swearing since they swear
only by the idol (an argument which would have made sense only to a
Jew who already argued that the idol meant nothing!).

The origin of image worship is explained euhemeristically (14.14-
21). Euhemerism is the theory named after Euhemerus of Messene, a
Greek writer who flourished about 300 BCE and wrote a story called
Sacred Writing about a fabulous utopian island called Panchaea in the
Indian Ocean. In it the kings and other rulers became deified after death
as Uranus, Cronus, Zeus, and the like. Euhemerism is frequent in Jewish writings of this general period because it was a way of asserting that
monotheism came first and that polytheism was only a corruption of
true worship. The Wisdom of Solomon asserts that it began with a father making an object of a beloved son who had died (14.15) The custom
was perpetuated by his descendants. Subjects made an image to remind
them of a distant ruler, and artists connived in this by making their
artwork even more flattering and attractive than the real thing. The
people were so tantalized by the beauty of the statue that they worshiped the image itself.

Particularly abhorrent to the writer is the worship of deities in the
image of various animals (12.23-27; 15.18–16.1). This was, of course,
the very form taken by many of the Egyptian gods, but the Jews were
not the only ones to find the practice loathsome. The Greeks and Romans, for all their polytheistic worship, found the Egyptian devotion to
animal-like deities disgusting. Juvenal, the Roman satirist of the early
second century CE, wrote about this as follows (*Satire* 15.1-10):

> Who knows not, O Bithynian Volusius, what monsters demented Egypt
> worships? One district adores the crocodile, aother venerates the ibis that
> gorges itself with snakes. In the place where magic chords are sounded by the
> truncated Memnon [a famous 'singing statue'], and ancient hundred gated

Thebes lies in ruins, men worship the glittering golden image of the long-tailed ape. In one part cats are worshipped, in another a river fish, in another whole townships venerate a dog; none adore Diana, but it is an impious outrage to crunch leeks and onions with the teeth. What a holy race to have such divinities springing up in their gardens!

Exclusivity/Inclusivity

An interesting question is the stance of the Wisdom of Solomon on the position of Gentiles in relationship to Jews. Are Gentiles simply beyond the pale, or is there some sort of accommodation of non-Jews into God's divine plan? Some passages definitely suggest an exclusivistic outlook. Wickedness is inborn into some, and despite the opportunity for repentance, God knows that they will not take the opportunity to do so (3.12; 12.3-11); evil disposition is predetermined. A similar concept occurs with regard to the Canaanites (12.3-11). This gets us into the area of determinism and free will which will be discussed below (pp. 61-63). For present purposes, the significant impression is that Gentiles (assuming they are the wicked—or at least are included in the category) are set in their corrupt ways, deserve only punishment and condemnation, and have nothing in common with God's people.

Thus, the initial perception is that the Wisdom of Solomon believes that the Jews should keep themselves aloof as a pure people, while the Gentiles are beyond redemption. Other passages are more ambiguous, however, suggesting that this scenario is only a part of the picture. The book begins by addressing the 'judges' (*krinontes*) of the earth and commanding them to love righteousness (1.1). The second section of the book begins by addressing the rulers of the earth (6.1-25). At first the writer seems unsympathetic and accuses the rulers of oppression and misrule and points out that they will be called to account (6.2-8). But then he proceeds to speak of how wisdom can guide the ruler and goes on to discuss the importance of obtaining her (6.9-11). This introductory session is followed by the rest of the chapters which extol the virtues and benefits of obtaining wisdom. The assumption seems to be, though, that the ruler who gains wisdom will rule rightly and well and gain much personally (cf. 6.21-25). This suggests that such rulers—even if Gentile—will gain favor in the sight of God. What is the point of finding wisdom if one is irrevocably condemned?

Wisdom is said to be *philanthrōpos* (1.6; 7.22-23), and the righteous person is similarly required to be *philanthrōpos* (12.19). The word means a 'lover of mankind', and the quality exhibited is that of *philanthrōpia* a'love of mankind'. The concept has a long history of discussion in Greek philosophy and ethics and would most likely have evoked some of this to a reader. The Stoics had long debated the question, arriving at a view well expressed by Cicero (*De Officiis* 1.50):

> The first principle is that which is found in the connection subsisting between all the members of the human race; and that bond of connection is reason and speech, which by the process of teaching and learning, of comunicating, discussing, and reasoning associate men together and unite them in a sort of natural fraternity.

A similar view is held by Philo, who refers to the concept of *philanthrōpia* at various points in his writings and devotes a good deal of his treatise *De Virtutibus* to the question. At his most direct, he can say in reference to Gen. 9.5 (*Quaest. in Gen.* 2.60):

> And (Scripture) calls 'brothers' those men who plot mischief, demon-strating...that all we men are kinsmen and brothers, being related by the possession of an ancient kinship, since we receive the lot of the rational nature from one mother.

Yet there is no question that Philo regards the Jewish law as essential, and he can describe the punishments of the enemies of Israel in graphic detail (*Praem. Poen.* 169-72). These differences can probably be recon-ciled through the thesis that Israel's law embodied universal principles for all humanity and that eventually all would be brought under its tutelage (cf. Winston 1984).

The same may be a way of explaining the apparent contradictions in the Wisdom of Solomon. The universalism is there, but it exists uneasily with a strong antipathy toward the Egyptians and other Gentiles. It has a lot to do with the doctrine of determinism in the Wis-dom of Solomon. If some Gentiles are predestined for corruption and condemnation, was it thought that some at least would embrace the Jewish law, learn heavenly wisdom, and become reconciled with God? It seems difficult to rule that out of the author's thinking. Few Jewish writings seem to rule out the idea of proselytes, and this would include the Wisdom of Solomon. But whether the writer's universalism went so far as accepting non-Jews apart from full conversion seems impossible to say from the statements in the book.

Determinism

In much of Jewish literature, a strong emphasis on individual choice and obedience, along with responsibility for one's own actions, exists side by side with statements suggesting God's arranging everything according to his divine will. Israel is God's chosen, yet they are constantly admonished to obey and not to forget the law. As Deuteronomy states, 'See, I have set before you today life and prosperity, death and adversity, if you obey the commandments of the Lord your God' (30.15-16). Yet God also 'hardens the heart' of individuals like Pharaoh (Exod. 8.15, 32, etc.) and Sihon king of the Amorites (Deut. 2.30). Apocalyptic literature contains many admonitions for readers, yet these writings often discuss God's plan in detail and imply that there is nothing anyone can do to change it. Most of the time there is little indication that the writers recognized a possible contradiction in the positions held.

At Qumran some texts imply that all mankind is divided into either 'the sons of light' or 'the sons of darkness'. Other texts are less black and white, however. For example, the astrological texts imply determinism—because you are born a certain way—but also suggest that one can have elements of both light and darkness in oneself (4Q186). Josephus makes a specific reference to a debate on the subject in Judaism (e.g., *War* 2.8.14 §§162-65):

> ...the Pharisees...attribute everything to Fate and to God; they hold that to act rightly or otherwise rests, indeed, for the most part with men, but that in each action Fate co-operates...The Sadducees...do away with Fate altogether, and remove God beyond, not merely the commission, but the very sight of evil. They maintain that man has the free choice of good or evil, and that it rests with each man's will whether he follows the one or the other.

An explicit debate over the issue arose in Greek literature, with various positions being taken as to whether free will, determinism, or something in between existed (see Winston 1979: 46-55 for a survey). Jewish tradition on the subject certainly found its way into the Wisdom of Solomon, though whether any of the Greek debate has influenced the writer is unclear.

There are statements suggesting a strong view about determinism. For example, wickedness seems to be an inherited trait (3.12); an evil disposition is predetermined. A similar concept occurs with regard to the Canaanites specifically (12.3-11). Their evil actions, real or imagined, are recounted in gleeful detail, as one might expect. It is also suggested that as a just deity, God gave the Canaanites the opportunity to repent so that no one could complain that he was unfair. And yet the book seems to express the belief that their deeds arise out of their inner qualities over which they have no control (3.10-11):

> But the ungodly will be punished as their reasoning deserves,
> those who disregarded the righteous
> and rebelled against the Lord;
> for those who despise wisdom and instruction are miserable.
> Their hope is in vain, their labors are unprofitable,
> and their works are useless.

As noted above (pp. 60-61), it is likely that the Wisdom of Solomon assumed that some Gentiles would have the opportunity for redemption, though they may have had to become Jews to receive it. Therefore, the universal predestination of Gentiles to damnation is probably not envisaged by the book. Whether his statements can be reconciled into a non-contradictory stance as Winston (1979: 58) argues is debatable. Although the writer does show knowledge of philosophy, there is no evidence that he addressed the issue from a philosophical point of view, nor should we necessarily expect such. This may mean that the writer did not comprehend the problems created by his various statements.

The Ideal of Kingship

Wisdom 6–10 presents a model for the reader to follow: Solomon as the ideal king (Mack 1973: 87-95; Reese 1970: 71-87; Kloppenborg 1982: 73-78) Granted, the writer of the book is never named, even though 'Solomon' is named in the headings of some manuscripts; hence the common name of the book, 'Wisdom of Solomon'. But even though not named, clearly the biblical Solomon is supposed to be speaking in the Book of Wisdom. This might seem a strange model to use, since few of the readers could expect to become rulers. There are several reasons why this was likely to have been important to the writer: the ultimate goal of the righteous was to rule with God; hence it was important that they cultivate kingly virtues. As well as the ideal king, Solomon is also the ideal sage (cf. p. 44 above), and many of the traits discussed are not limited to rulers. All should seek wisdom, for example, not just monarchs.

So all readers are drawn into the circle created by 'Solomon', the supposed author of the book. He addresses the rulers of the earth in ch. 6, then he begins an autobiographical narrative in ch. 7. He describes his birth and upbringing, emphasizing the process of birth and growing experienced in common with all men; in this kings are no different from their subjects. Solomon now shifts to the subject of wisdom, her characteristics and benefits (7.7–8.16). Wis. 7.7–9.18 is devoted to Solomon's quest for wisdom.

The writer seems to be influenced by the literary genre of treatises *On Kingship* (Reese 1970: 72-78). A number of these were written in antiquity, often addressed to a particular king. Interestingly, they seldom discuss the problems and realities of actual rulership but are often simply a vehicle for the writer's discourses on a particular subject, especially morality. They frequently present a model of human perfection. The imprint of this sort of tract on the Wisdom of Solomon can be seen in two ways: (a) God is presented in a universal, cosmopolitan sense, not as the particular God of Israel; (b) the just man is exhibited in an analytical way (contrary to the Old Testament tradition) and is referred to as 'man' (*anthrōpos*), not in a specifically Jewish way. 'Solomon' makes the point of his origins like those of any other person (7.1-6). Hellenistic philosophers often admonished rulers on avoiding pride and recognizing their common humanity with their subjects.

Kloppenborg (1982: 73-78) agrees with Reese about the importance of the Hellenistic kingly ideal, but he argues that there is considerable influence from the Isis cult. Solomon's search for wisdom is paralleled by Isis's relationship with the Ptolemaic king. For example, wisdom is espoused both to God (8.3) and to the king (8.9). The same applies to Isis who is the wife of (the murdered) Osiris but also the royal spouse and mistress of the royal household. For a further discussion about Isis influence, see pp. 79-80 and 92-93.

Cosmology and Nature

Nature—physics in the ancient sense—plays a large role in the Wisdom of Solomon. There a number of references to nature and the value of knowledge about it. It is one of the characteristics (and gifts) of wisdom (Wis. 7.17-22):

> For it is he who gave me unerring knowledge of what exists,
> to know the structure of the world and the activity of the elements;
> the beginning and end and middle of times,
> the alternations of the solstices and the changes of the seasons,
> the cycles of the year and the constellations of the stars,
> the natures of animals and the tempers of wild animals,
> the powers of spirits and the thoughts of human beings,
> the varieties of plants and the virtues of roots;
> I learned both what is secret and what is manifest,
> for wisdom, the fashioner of all things, taught me.

This interest in *Listenwissenschaft* (science of lists, which is one way of organizing knowledge in all ages) and encyclopaedic learning is characteristic of the wisdom literature of the ancient Near East. To be wise meant knowing about the natural world, the mysteries of plants and animals, the movements of the heavens, and the workings of the cosmos. The Wisdom of Solomon shows the interests of the author by mentioning them in passing, but they are not dwelt on in detail. Yet as already noted (pp. 42-43) the writer seems to draw on contemporary scientific knowledge about the elements, as understood in the Greco–Roman world, in developing the significance of the plagues of Egypt. This comes out further in a couple of passages, such as 11.17:

> For your all-powerful hand,
> which created the world out of formless matter [*ex amorphou hulēs*]...

Here the writer seems to be assuming that the world was created from pre-existing but unformed matter, a view widely held by the Greeks. For example, Plato's dialogue on the origin of the world likewise speaks of the 'unformed' (*amorphon*) nature of the original substance shaped by the creator (*Timaeus* 50d). A similar statement occurs in Aristotle (*Physics* 191a, 10). The Wisdom of Solomon does not seem to have anything else in mind. The idea that the elements formed matter and could be interchanged as a part of creation was a widespread view. The Wisdom of Solomon states (19.6, 19):

> For the whole creation in its nature was fashioned anew,
> complying with your commands,
> so that your children might be kept unharmed...
> For land animals were transformed into water creatures,
> and creatures that swim moved over to the land.

Similar statements can be found in philosophical writings. For example, Cicero writes (*De Natura Deorum* 3.39.92):

Nor do you say this as some superstitious fable or old wives' tale, but you give a scientific and systematic account of it: you allege that matter, which constitutes and contains all things, is in its entirety flexible and subject to change, so that there is nothing that cannot be moulded and transmuted out of it however suddenly...

But what of belief in *creatio ex nihilo*—creation out of nothing? The question of when this belief arose has been much debated in recent years (Winston 1971–72; Goldstein 1984; Winston 1986; Goldstein 1987). Some statements in rabbinic literature seem to point in that direction, though their precise connotation is disputed. In any case, such

statements are found in literature well after the first century CE and an
earlier origin for them cannot be taken for granted. The first clear belief
in *creatio ex nihilo* seems to be second-century Christianity (Tatian, *To
the Greeks* 5; Theophilus of Antioch 2.4.10), if Winston is correct
(1971–72). In any case, the author of the Wisdom of Solomon does not
seem to hold such a belief.

Apologetic on Behalf of the Jews

Apologetic is found in various Jewish writings of this period. One of
the best examples is Josephus's *Antiquities* (as is also his *Against Apion*,
from a different perspective). The main concern of the Wisdom of
Solomon does not seem to be primarily apologetic. However, there are
several passges where the writer seems to want to defend aspects of
Judaism. What this might say about the audience will be considered on
pp. 91-94.

When the writer deals with the Canaanites, he seems to feel the need
to justify their being driven from the land (12.3-18). He does this by
arguing that they forfeited any right to it by their abominable deeds.
The Old Testament already alludes to this (Leviticus 18; Deut. 18.9-
14), but the Wisdom of Solomon embellishes to the furthest extent by
accusing them of child murder, cannibalism, and unspeakable rites. He
appears to be going beyond any need for pure description and seems
almost ashamed of what was done to the original inhabitants of the
land. The theme of the land and the right to it was an important issue
in literature of the Hasmonean period (Mendels 1987). Although the
Wisdom of Solomon does not indicate that it is caught up in a current
debate, as was the case when the Hasmoneans were actively conquering
territory, the author seems to recognize that the biblical account of the
conquest of Canaan does not present the Jews in a good light.

At least one other example of apology can be found in the book. The
writer makes a brief reference to the bronze serpent erected by Moses
(16.5-10). This is just after he has spent two chapters lambasting the
worship of idols and animals. Is he completely unaware of the conflict
with his previous argument, that it badly undermines the logic of his
attack on images? One suspects that he was at least somewhat uneasy
because he avoids mentioning the bronze image directly, and he makes
the point that it was God who did the healing rather than the image.
But what pagan would have thought otherwise!

Further Reading

The commentaries, such as those of Winston (1979) and Larcher (1983–85), give information on the theology and message of the book. Other standard reference works provide summaries, including Pfeiffer (1949: Introduction); Nickelsburg (1981); and Gilbert (1986). Other studies on individual subjects and passages include Collins (1977-78:. 121-42); Gilbert (1973; 1984); Kloppenborg (1982:. 57-84); Kolarcik (1991); Mack (1973); Reese (1970); Winston (1971–72: 185-202). On the idea of immortality versus resurrection as 'characteristic' of Jewish eschatology, see Barr (1966). The standard treatment of eschatology in early Judaism remains Nickelsburg (1972).

On the importance of the land and the views about it in Jewish literature of this general period, see the following (though the Wisdom of Solomon is not treated): Mendels (1987).

The bibliography on apocalypticism is huge. A discussion of some of the primary sources and secondary literature, as well as the worldview relating to it, is found in Collins (1977–78) and the following works: Collins (1974: 21-43; 1984); Grabbe (1996: ch. 4).

4

THE FIGURE OF WISDOM

Introduction

The figure of wisdom has a long history in Judaism. It first makes its appearance in the book of Proverbs. The precedents of and influences on the presentation of Dame Wisdom or Lady Wisdom in Proverbs 1–9 are debated, and we shall be looking at some of the theories offered. For example, many have compared wisdom in Proverbs with the goddess Maat in Egypt. Whereas wisdom in Proverbs 8 emphasizes her own accessibility, the beautiful poem on wisdom in Job 28 sees it as hidden and difficult to find, an entity which must be sought out with great labor. In Ben Sira 24 wisdom searches for a resting place among mankind and finds it in Israel, but in 1 Enoch 42 she finds no resting place and finally returns to heaven.

Alongside the evolution of Dame Wisdom is the idea of the logos (from the Greek word for 'discourse, reason'). This also has a long history in both Judaism and Greco–Roman culture. It culminates in the logos concept found in Philo of Alexandria and in the identification of Jesus with the logos in the Gospel of John. This figure of wisdom in the Wisdom of Solomon did not arise in a vacuum; behind it lie centuries of development and influences from both the Greek and the Semitic side. The history of the figure of wisdom provides part of the context of wisdom in the Wisdom of Solomon and needs to be considered alongside the information in the book itself. In its turn, the figure of wisdom in the Wisdom of Solomon represents an important stage in the development of the concept.

We find two models of wisdom in the tradition. Both are personifications but with separate images. One of these is that of a goddess-like figure; the other is that of seducer or lover or erotic figure. Not every source has both images, but several do, including the Wisdom of Solomon.

Early Development of the Figure

Proverbs

The central passage on the figure of wisdom is Proverbs 8, though there are important contributions in chs. 1, 7, and 9. How early these passages are is debated. Most consider Proverbs 1–9 postexilic (cf. Maier 1995); however, it has been argued that there is nothing to prevent these chapters from being pre-exilic (Kayatz 1966). A lot turns on one's view of the development of theology and wisdom in Israel rather than specific indications in the chapters themselves. In any case, many of the later discussions about the figure of wisdom contain allusions to data in ch. 8 and other chapters in Proverbs 1–9.

In Prov. 1.20-33, wisdom cries aloud in the streets, rebuking the scoffers and dunces for not heeding her call. She will laugh when misfortune comes on them because of their refusal to heed her. Willful ignorance will bear fruit of an unpleasant kind. In ch. 8, wisdom delivers more than one speech. Her first speech in 8.1-11 is similar to that in ch. 1: she calls on all to hear—the dullards included—because her discipline is better than silver. Prov. 8.12-21 continues with this theme, pointing out the benefits to be had from love of wisdom, not just for the lowly but also for kings and nobles.

Prov. 8.22-34 is a passage of prime importance, because in it wisdom is closely identified with Yahweh. She was begotten at the beginning, even before the foundations of the earth were laid. She was an observer of God's work of creation, and even his *'āmôn*. The meaning of this Hebrew word in 8.30 has puzzled commentators for centuries (cf. Whybray 1994: 134-36). Some translate it as 'technician' (perhaps in the sense of 'architect'); others see it as 'confidant' (NJPS) or even as 'child'. If the term means 'architect', wisdom was not only present but even a part of the creation process. In any case, she is presented as an intimate of Yahweh and with a privileged position.

Proverbs 9 contrasts Lady Wisdom, who has prepared a feast with an open invitation for any to partake of, with the foolish woman—Dame Folly (presented in the image of a prostitute)—who invites the foolish into her house only to bring them down to Sheol (cf. Maier 1995). The imagery is intriguing here. That Dame Folly is configured as a prostitute is what one would expect, considering that she is expected to be viewed negatively. Lady Wisdom also appears as a seductress. This is logical pairing with Dame Folly, but it presents problems because 'nice girls' were not supposed to practice seduction, as far as we know. Only 'bad' women displayed their feminine charms publicly. The writer has used an image which fits the context logically but would not have fitted Israelite society. Her aims are of the purest, of course, but the imagery used is that of seduction, even if the emphasis of the literal text is on food rather than the physical charms of the hostess (9.2-5):

> She has slaughtered her animals, she has mixed her wine,
> > she has also set her table.
> She has sent out her servant girls, she calls
> > from the highest places in the town,
> 'You that are simple, turn in here!'
> > To those without sense she says,
> 'Come, eat of my bread and drink of the wine I have mixed.'

Job 28

This beautiful poem gives a picture in marked contrast to that in Proverbs, at least in one aspect. Whereas Proverbs makes the point of how readily wisdom can be sought out and found, Job 28 emphasizes her inaccessibility. Only with great difficulty, and only with God's help, can wisdom be reached. Precious metals are found in hidden places of the earth and can be dug out in remote regions only with effort. But wisdom is even less reachable. The ocean deep does not know it. Even the place of the dead has only heard a rumor of its location. God alone who sees everything, even to the ends of the earth, has searched it out. Wisdom is within reach but only through God (28.20-24):

> Where then does wisdom come from?
> > And where is the place of understanding?
> It is hidden from the eyes of all living,
> > and concealed from the birds of the air.
> Abaddon and Death say,
> > 'We have heard a rumor of it with our ears.'
> God understands the way to it,
> > and he knows its place.
> For he looks to the ends of the earth,
> > and sees everything under the heavens.

Ben Sira

Ben Sira (Ecclesiasticus) 24 has a good deal in common with Proverbs 8. Wisdom speaks in the assembly of the Most High, praising herself. She came forth from his mouth and abode in the highest heavens.

Then, she moved over all the earth, looking for a dwelling place among mankind (24.6-12):

> Over the waves of the sea, over all the earth,
>> and over every people and nation I have held sway.
> Among all these I sought a resting place;
>> in whose territory should I abide?
> Then the Creator of all things gave me a command,
>> and my Creator chose the place for my tent.
> He said, 'Make your dwelling in Jacob,
>> and in Israel receive your inheritance.'
>
> Thus in the beloved city he gave me a resting place,
>> and in Jerusalem was my domain.
> I took root in an honored people,
>> in the portion of the Lord, his heritage.

Here she flourishes and grows, and calls those who desire her to come and eat their fill. She is then identified with God's law, the Torah (v. 23):

> All this is the book of the covenant of the Most High God,
>> the law that Moses commanded us
>> as an inheritance for the congregations of Jacob.

The image of wisdom in Ben Sira is one in which she is accessible but only to Israel. The rest of the world does not enjoy her presence; it is Israel who possesses her in the form of the Torah.

The erotic image of wisdom is found in Sir. 51.13-30. The Greek text was the only form of the book known for many centuries. Portions of the Hebrew original were discovered a century ago. Some more fragments have now been found among the Dead Sea Scrolls. A comparison of the Greek and Hebrew texts suggests that the translator toned down language which seems to be more explicitly erotic in the Hebrew text. The discovery of this text in the Psalms scroll from Qumran Cave 11 (11QPs^a) has helped to make clear the original nature of the poem. The author's courting of wisdom is expressed in the language of lovemaking. Some of the passages now thought to demonstrate this erotic language are the following (in the translation of J.A. Sanders, whose 1967 study should be seen for a justification of this interpretation):

> I was a young man before I had erred
>> when I looked for her.
> She came to me in her beauty
>> when finally I sought her out.

> I purposed to make sport:
>> I was zealous for pleasure,
>> without pause.
> I kindled my desire for her
>> without distraction.
> I bestirred my desire for her
>> and on her heights I do not waver.
> I spread my hand(s)…
>> and perceive her unseen parts.

1 Baruch

The book of 1 Baruch, difficult to date but probably from the second century BCE, has a section on wisdom (3.15–4.4). It stresses the inaccessibility of wisdom and the fact that she was not available to the various nations who sought her (3.20-23). Only God, the one who knows all things and who created them, knows how to find her (3.31-32). But he found her and gave her to Israel; indeed, she is identical to his law (3.36–4.1):

> He found the whole way to knowledge,
>> and gave her to his servant Jacob
>> and to Israel, whom he loved.
> Afterward she appeared on earth and lived with humankind.
> She is the book of the commandments of God,
>> the law that endures forever.
> All who hold her fast will live,
>> and those who forsake her will die.

1 Enoch 42

Some have thought that 1 Enoch preserves an old myth of wisdom as a goddess. Although this is not clearly the case, we find here another version of wisdom's quest for a place among humans (42.1-3, Knibb's 1978 translation):

> Wisdom found no place where she could dwell, and her dwelling was in heaven. Wisdom went out in order to dwell among the sons of men, but did not find a dwelling; wisdom returned to her place and took her seat in the midst of the angels. And iniquity came out from her chambers; those whom she did not seek she found, and dwelt among them, like rain in the desert, and like dew on parched ground.

The Parables of Enoch (1 En. 37–71) are generally considered the latest section of the book. Although the dating is controversial, quite a few specialists put this section in the first century CE. In this version, wisdom maintains her place in the Divine Council after finding no resting place on earth, though presumably she is accessible to those who are worthy.

The Background of the Figure of Wisdom

The source of the picture in Proverbs has been much debated. Is it a native development? Is it borrowed from abroad, from Egypt or Mesopotamia? How is this figure to be conceived? A personification? A mythical figure? A hypostasis? A variety of answers have been given to these questions.

William F. Albright argued that wisdom was originally a Canaanite goddess, which accounts for 'Canaanite' features in the Dame Wisdom of Proverbs. For evidence of this he refers to the writing of Ahiqar. Although Ahiqar was originally a traditional Near Eastern tale of the first millennium BCE, it has been 'Judaized' and become a part of Jewish literature. According to Albright (1919–20), Ahiqar 94–95 is to be translated as follows:

> [Wi]sdom is [from] the gods, and to the gods she is precious; for[ever] her kingdom is fixed in he[av]en for the holy lord (lit. lord of the holy things) elevated [her - - -].

Most subsequent translations have been along the same lines. In the most recent edition (Porten and Yardeni 1993), the fragments have been slightly rearranged so that the first part of the quote ('wisdom is from the gods') is no longer a part of the context; nevertheless, the editors still take the subject of 'she' as wisdom, and the sense is thus similar to that given to it by earlier editors.

The difficulty, though, is that the passage does not support Albright's contention. He has to assume that 'wisdom' has displaced the name of a Canaanite goddess. Unfortunately, there is no evidence for such a Canaanite goddess. If wisdom is indeed the subject of the statement, it is not clearly different from the figure of wisdom in the Jewish writings in question.

The figure of wisdom is often seen as a personification. Another term sometimes used is 'hypostasis', which means an extreme form of personification in which the personified figure represents the deity but is also seen as having an existence in its own right. Although the logos becomes hypostasized in some theological systems (e.g., Philo of Alexandria), the term should probably not be used in the early development of the figure of wisdom. Hengel (1974) uses 'hypostasis' of the figure in Proverbs, but most would be against this usage of the term. Rather we must reckon with personification of some sort (cf. Whybray 1965), and there is widespread agreement that in Dame Wisdom of Proverbs we find some sort of personification. The question is, personification of what? Just an abstract concept or is there more to it? Personification explains some of the features of wisdom, but not all; she has divine features which cannot be clarified by this explanation. Indeed, she appears in some passages as nothing less than a goddess.

Recently, Bernhard Lang has returned to the idea of an Israelite goddess as the model for Lady Wisdom in Proverbs 8. The description of wisdom can easily be considered a goddess figure here. In line with a good deal of recent thinking, Lang points to the fact that monotheism developed only late in Israel, and a goddess may well have been a part of Israel's pantheon during its earlier polytheistic phase. The existence of an Israelite goddess is mainly an inference, but there is some direct evidence in the recent discovery of inscriptions which seem to mention a female consort for YHWH (Dever 1984 and Zevit 1984, though surprisingly Lang rejects the interpretation which would support his thesis [1986: 171 n. 8]).

Lang has also appealed to the model of the wisdom teacher or school pedagogue for the figure in Prov. 1.20-33, with overtones in chs. 8 and 9. Wisdom appears as a teacher, and he feels this image comes from schools within Israel. (The goddess features, to his mind, come from the fact that abstract qualities are often deified.) The problem is that there is a fierce debate on the question of schools, and many argue there is no evidence for formal schools in ancient Israel (cf. Grabbe 1995b: 190-96). Scribes could have been trained by a system of apprenticeship, while the idea of universal schooling is very much an anachronism from nineteenth-century Western thinking. Wisdom could be pictured as a teacher without thinking of the pedagogue of a formal school.

The model which has perhaps the widest following is to see Dame Wisdom as a personification but with mythical features (Whybray 1965: 76-95; Kayatz 1966). The goddess features are usually thought to come from the goddess Maat. The name of the divinity comes from the Egyptian word *m3'.t* meaning 'order, wisdom, truth, righteousness'. In the famous pictures of the judgment scene found in the Egyptian *Book of the Dead* (ch. 125), Maat has an important function. The soul is brought before Osiris by her. The soul is weighed in the balance in which Maat (or Maat's symbol in the form of an ostrich feather) is in the other pan of the scales. Thus, the soul's integrity and deeds are measured against the standard of Maat and judged accordingly.

The case for Maat as the model for Dame Wisdom is given by C. Kayatz (1966). In Proverbs 8 wisdom speaks. The direct address of God, 'I am YHWH', in various passages (e.g., Gen. 26.4; Exod. 3.6; Lev. 19.12, 26; Isa. 43.11) has often been appealed to as the precedent for this. Indeed, wisdom speaks in the first person in many ways similarly to the way God speaks; however, there are some differences. The main one, according to Kayatz, is that wisdom speaks in a timeless, cosmic context, whereas YHWH speaks of past historical events and makes pronouncements that a new historically based salvation is beginning (85). To Kayatz this difference is decisive. Whether one can make such a neat distinction between the 'historical' and the 'cosmic' is debatable, but Kayatz goes on to argue that the self-predication speeches of various Egyptian gods and goddesses show a closer correspondence to the speech of wisdom in Proverbs 8 (Maat does not come into the picture here because she never speaks herself). (However, Lang [1986: 60] compares the speech of Ishtar in Mesopotamia and states that the 'goddess of the king' is common in the ancient Near East.)

Prov. 8.22-31 describes wisdom's place at creation. She was with God in the beginning before anything else was created. In a speech of Atum (*Coffin Texts* 2.80), Maat is pictured as being with the creator (Atum) before anything else existed. She is his daughter and is pictured as a child (Kayatz 1966: 93-96). The love between wisdom and mankind is described in several passages (8.17, 20-21, 34). Maat is also mentioned as one who loves or is loved (Kayatz 1966: 99-102). In many cases, the subject or object is a god, but sometimes it is the king. The gods live through Maat (Kayatz 1966: 105), just as wisdom gives life and protection (1.33; 3.16, 18; 8.35). Maat (and other gods) are sometimes pictured with the *ankh* symbol which stands for life. Wisdom is an ornament around the neck (1.9; 3.3, 32; 6.21); similarly, the Maat symbol was worn on a neck chain by the vizier and the high judges, and was generally pictured as a neck ornament (Kayatz 1966: 108-109). Wisdom and her teaching gives a crown to the head (1.9; 4.9). Maat is pictured both as being a crown and as granting a crown (Kayatz 1966: 111-17). According to Prov. 8.15-16 kingship is founded on 'righteousness' (Hebrew ṣdq). Pictures from ancient Egypt show the throne daïs of the king with the Maat symbol (Brunner 1958). Both literally and metaphorically the kingship rests upon Maat.

To accept this thesis of a connection with Maat does not mean that a direct borrowing has to be postulated (though it might be one possibility). For example, Kayatz does not argue for 'a direct takeover of

Maat thinking and the Maat concept into Israelite wisdom thinking, but the essential and relational determinations of wisdom are the result of a thorough-going assimilation' (1966: 138). As will be discussed below (pp. 79-80), in time Maat seems to be assimilated to and taken over by the goddess Isis. As the wife of Osiris and the mother of Horus, Isis was always an important figure in the Egyptian pantheon. It is hardly surprising that Maat eventually becomes assimilated to the dominant goddess.

How are we to evaluate these different suggestions? None of the hypotheses mentioned above can be considered as demonstrated. Some are plausible, but plausibility is not proof. Lang has demonstrated that in its polytheistic period, Israel *might* have had a goddess by the name of 'Wisdom' or analogous to wisdom. On the other hand, although no direct connection with Egyptian Maat has been demonstated, the image of Maat has many close parallels with the passages on wisdom, especially Proverbs 8. No one has shown that the figure of wisdom must have been modeled on or influenced by Maat, yet it fits very well. This is as far as we can go in our present state of knowledge. The choice of one explanation over the other is very subjective.

The Logos Tradition

Wisdom is the main personification or hypostasis found in many Jewish writings. However, in some writings the dominant concept used is that of logos rather than wisdom. For example, in Philo the logos is a central concept in his philosophical and theological system. Wisdom (*sophia*) certainly occurs, but it plays a less prominent role. The place of wisdom in other writings is taken by the logos in Philo, even if there is inevitably a certain overlap between the two.

For Philo, God is beyond being and beyond unity—ultimately unknowable—but he uses the expression *to ōn* 'the one who is' for the deity. God is transcendent and has no direct dealings with the world. But an emanation comes from him like a stream of light which reaches toward the world and makes him emanent and accessible to humanity. The first stage of the emanation is referred to as the logos. It then divides into two powers, the creative power and royal power. In some treatments there is a further bifurcation. Each of the stages is progressively less pure. Thus, God maintains his unity and purity, but the gap is bridged by the logos.

The logos can be referred to as a hypostasis. In some contexts, it is referred to as 'God' and 'son of God', but at other times it is treated as a separate being. Although wisdom (*sophia*) occurs much less frequently, it is treated as more or less equivalent to the logos. Sometimes *sophia* is considered the parent of the logos, but in the same context logos also generates wisdom (*Fug.* 97, 108-109). The overall impression is that logos and *sophia* are equivalent for Philo, but for some reason he prefers the term logos.

The logos concept has a long history in Greco–Roman thought. Already in the fourth century BCE the Stoics used logos to refer to the intelligence of the cosmos—in some ways equivalent to 'God'. The universe was co-extensive with God, but the logos gave it guidance and intellect. It was the 'reason' or 'mind' of God.

Some have seen a connection between logos and the 'word of the Lord' in the Old Testament. Logos of course means 'discourse' as well as 'mind, reason'. In the theology of the Old Testament itself the word does not play a central part. There are times when God's word is slightly personified, but it is primarily in later Jewish literature that the word takes on features of personification. It is the use of the Aramaic *memra'* 'word' in the Targums that has often been drawn on to explain a Jewish or Semitic background to the logos concept. The difficulty is the lateness of the Targums which use the word in its most interesting form, especially the Targum Pseudo-Jonathan. The present form of Pseudo-Jonathan is post-Islamic. Some think that it comes from 'a Palestinian Targum' of a much earlier time. The matter is debated, with some scholars arguing for a pre-70 Palestinian Targum, which is the basis of Targum Pseudo-Jonathan and Targum Neofiti, and others strongly opposing it. Therefore, the precise relevance of *memra'* to the logos concept has yet to be determined.

Wisdom in the Book of Wisdom

Characteristics of Wisdom

The figure of wisdom in the Wisdom of Solomon is found primarily in chs. 6–12 but can be said to lie behind chs. 13–19 as well, though these refer directly to God. She appears in both the guises discussed above, that of a heavenly figure and that of an erotic image. The writer, in the guise of Solomon, extols the benefits from seeking wisdom (chs. 6–7).

Wisdom is closely associated with God, and the relationship is a fascinating one. As already noted, that which is considered the activity of wisdom in Wisdom 10 gradually shifts to that of God in Wisdom 11

and following. Wisdom is the mother of all things (7.12); she is the
fashioner (*technitis*) of all things (7.22). In 7.15-20 God is the guide of
wisdom, and he also gives knowledge with regard to the cycles of
nature and the world. Yet similar characteristics are ascribed to wisdom
in 8.5-8. The relationship is most clearly expressed in 7.25-26:

> For she is a breath of the power of God,
> and a pure emanation of the glory of the Almighty;
> therefore nothing defiled gains entrance into her.
> For she is a reflection of eternal light,
> a spotless mirror of the working of God,
> and an image of his goodness.

This statement seems to fit the interpretation usually given that wisdom
in the Wisdom of Solomon is a *hypostasis*. That is, she is both product
of God and also a manifestation of him. She represents him and she is
him. Thus, many statements about God are interchangeable with statements about wisdom.

The characteristics of wisdom are ultimately those we would also
apply to God (7.22-23):

> There is in her a spirit that is intelligent, holy,
> unique, manifold, subtle,
> mobile, clear, unpolluted,
> distinct, invulnerable, loving the good, keen,
> irresistible, beneficent, humane,
> steadfast, sure, free from anxiety,
> all-powerful, overseeing all,
> and penetrating through all spirits
> that are intelligent, pure, and altogether subtle.

More than this, these are also the characteristics which humans should
strive for. This leads immediately to the central motif to which the author of the Wisdom of Solomon draws attention. This is the function
of wisdom as a teacher.

'Solomon' sought wisdom because she brought wisdom and understanding to him personally (7.7-14). She teaches the four cardinal virtues
(8.7; cf. p. 38); she knows the past and can foresee the future, and she
understands riddles and clever speech (8.8). Because of her good
counsel, one can gain honor, glory, and respect over others; one's peers,
elders, and even kings will admire and defer to one's judgment (8.9-12).
She gives the ability to rule and cause monarchs to fear the one who
possesses her because of skill in war (8.14-16). Most of all, though, she
brings immortality to the possessor and everlasting remembrance of him
(8.13, 17).

Erotic language is not very conspicuous, but it occurs here and there. Several times mention is made of those who 'love' her (6.12, 17-18). Other such language is found in 8.2-3:

> I loved her and sought her from my youth;
> I desired to take her for my bride,
> and became enamored of her beauty.
> She glorifies her noble birth by living with God,
> and the Lord of all loves her.

Recent Study on Wisdom in the Wisdom of Solomon

A number of scholars have seen the background of wisdom in the Wisdom of Solomon in the Isis aretalogies (Mack 1973: 63-107; Reese 1970: 36-50; Kloppenborg 1982). The native Isis cult of ancient Egypt had been exported widely over the Mediterranean world in the Hellenistic period. Instead of just being a part of the native worship in Egyptian temples, it now became a universal mystery religion in which non-Egyptian converts were initiated into its mysteries and worshiped at local Isis temples. Many poems in honor of Isis were written, referred to as Isis aretalogies. Some of these have been preserved and show parallels to wisdom as described in the Wisdom of Solomon. Most of those preserved are in Greek.

Reese has suggested that Jewish youth were being attracted to Isis worship. By drawing on features of the Isis cult, the Wisdom of Solomon thought to counter these influences and attract the Jewish youth back to their own people and religion. Regardless of whether this interpretation is correct (see pp. 92-93 below for an evaluation), the writer could well have been making using of the Isis tradition to construct the figure of wisdom. There are a number of indications in this regard.

Wisdom is presented as a savior (Kloppenborg 1982: 67-73). This imagery is new to the Israelite wisdom tradition. Although wisdom has many characteristics, as noted above, there are no references to her as savior; this seems to be reserved for God. Although the Greek noun 'savior' (*sōtēr*) is not used, the verb (*sōzō*) certainly is (9.18). She is a mediator figure (8.2-9). She guarded the first man created (10.1). She preserved Abraham blameless (10.5); she saved Lot (10.6); she delivered all those who served her (10.9): the righteous Joseph from sin (10.13), the devout people and blameless seed from a nation of oppressors (10.15), and so on. As Kloppenborg notes (1982: 72):

What is distinctive in the Wisdom of Solomon is (1) the *saving role* of Sophia
[Wisdom], corresponding to Isis's major function; (2) the *selection of events*
which the author used as examples of this role; and (3) the *allusive re-telling* of
these events in such a way that they resonate with the *mythic pattern* characteristic of the Isis–Horus cycle. The biblical account is thereby allowed to
participate in the *mythic power* of the symbol of a savior deity, but without
acquiring the explicit aspects of the Egyptian myth.

The Wisdom of Solomon brings together the wisdom tradition and
the logos tradition. It also brings together the 'near' wisdom and the
'hidden' wisdom traditions, as for example in 8.21. With the addition
of the Isis imagery just described the Wisdom of Solomon has developed the figure of wisdom in an imaginative way to meet the needs of
contemporary Jewish thinking. What this may say about the audience
of the book is addressed in the next chapter.

Further Reading

An important study of the development of the concepts of wisdom and logos is Mack
(1973); see also Ringgren (1947); Marcus (1950–51: 157-71).

Treatments of Dame Wisdom in Proverbs are found in Albright (1919–20: 258-94);
Brunner (1958: 426-28); Hengel (1974); Kayatz (1966); Lang (1986); Maier (1995);
Whybray (1965; 1994).

The definitive edition of Ahiqar is now found in Porten and Yardeni (1993).

On the question of schools in Israel, see the summary of the debate, with bibliography,
in Grabbe (1995: 190-96). A recent study on Maat is Lichtheim (1992).

For a translation of 1 Enoch, see Knibb (1978); Sparks (1984).

On the inscriptions which suggest that Yahweh may have had a consort, see Dever
(1984: 21-37); Zevit (1984: 39-47).

For arguments that 11QPs[a] and Ben Sira 51 contain erotic language, see Sanders (1967).

For an introduction to Philo of Alexandria, including his logos concept, see Goodenough
(1962); Sandmel (1979).

For an introduction to Stoic beliefs, including their concept of logos, and other
Hellenistic philosophies, see Long (1974).

On the problems with dating the Targums, which is an important factor in evaluating the
use of 'word' (*memra*') as background for personification of wisdom, see Grabbe (1979:
393-401).

On the figure of wisdom in the Wisdom of Solomon, see Mack (1973: 63–107) and
Kloppenborg (1982: 57-84).

5

THE HISTORICAL CONTEXT

Introduction

Rather than beginning with the historical context and a discussion of time, place, and authorship, we have so far remained within the book itself. We have looked at the content, genre, structure, rhetoric, and theology of the book. Now, we are in a position to lift our eyes to wider horizons and to ask when and where the book was written and by whom. These questions have not been ignored up to now because they are unimportant; on the contrary, they are very important, but it is because of their significance that they can be pursued only after the necessary groundwork has been laid.

To begin to answer these questions, we need to compare the characteristics of the book with what is known of Jewish history and society at the time. But the Wisdom of Solomon could possibly have been written at any point during a broad span of time and over a wide area of Jewish settlement. Rather than beg the question, we must first survey the history of the Jewish communities at the potential times and places of writing.

A Survey of Jewish History

Introduction

In 334 BCE Alexander led an army across the sea to Asia Minor and changed the Near East forever. He moved down the Mediterranean coast to Egypt, during which time he would have received the submission of Judah, then eastward to Iran. The final defeat of the Persians came at Gaugamela in 331. But Alexander did not stop there. He pushed on eastward, into modern Afghanistan and finally northern

India by 328, before his troops decided they had had enough and refused to go further. Greek rule now extended over the entire ancient Near East and even further. It covered mainland Greece, Thrace, Asia Minor, Syro-Palestine, Egypt, Mesopotamia, Iran, Afghanistan, and even a portion of India.

When Alexander died prematurely in 323, his extensive conquests had not been consolidated. For the next 40 years, his generals (the Diadochi) fenced, maneuvered, formed and broke alliances, and fought one another for control of the vast land mass now under Greek control. Their armies marched, battled, and plundered throughout the area. We know little about the Jews during this period, though Palestine and its inhabitants certainly would not have escaped the ravages of this time. In any case, the centuries-long process of Hellenization had already begun.

The coming of the Greeks and the Hellenization of the ancient Near East marks the beginning of the time when the Wisdom of Solomon might have been written. Alexander established the Hellenistic world from the beginning as a synthesis of new Greek elements and the millennia-old characteristics of the ancient Near Eastern empires. Hellenization was neither Greek nor Oriental—or rather it was both—it was *sui generis*. Some things changed, much remained the same; Greek cultural elements were added to the culture rather than displacing the native. The new creation was a complex entity that continued to develop and evolve until the Arab conquest.

The Ptolemies

Jews settled in Egypt from an early period, probably as early as the time of the Diadochi. According to one story, the high priest Ezechius (Hezekiah) led a group of Jews into Egypt, probably under Ptolemy I. The Jewish settlements seemed to have continued without interruption until the second century CE, though they experienced a series of ups and downs (see below). In 301 Palestine itself came under Ptolemaic rule and remained so for a century, until Antiochus III took it away in 200 BCE. Specific information on the Jews of Palestine comes only episodically. The Ptolemies put their own tax and administrative system into place, but it seems to have been only an adaption of that used by the Persians. The province of Judah evidently continued much as it had under Persian rule, though there were some differences.

The Greeks made use of military colonies (*cleruchies*), especially in border regions, to help police and intimidate the native population, as well as to settle veterans. From the Zenon papyri we know that Tobias, a Jewish local leader, headed a military colony centered on Araq el-Emir across the Jordan. Preserved are letters from Tobias to high administrative officials in Egypt and even to the Ptolemaic king himsef. Although these letters are in Greek, they were no doubt written by Greek scribes in Tobias's service, so we cannot be sure that he knew that language. On the other hand, even if Tobias himself did not read Greek, his descendants evidently did. The story of Tobias's son (or grandson) Joseph and his sons is of a family at home in the Greek-speaking world and even the Ptolemaic royal court.

In Egypt itself, the position of the Jews is only sporadically attested (see the survey in Tcherikover *et al.* 1957–64: 19-25). According to 3 Maccabees, the Jewish community was threatened with death under Ptolemy IV, shortly after the battle of Raphia in 217 BCE. Josephus also makes allegations of persecutions, but there is little evidence to support these. Putting together the brief information we have suggests that the Jews enjoyed considerable favor during the reign of Ptolemy VI Philometor (180–145 BCE), no doubt for political reasons (including rivalries in the ruling family itself). When Ptolemy VIII Euergetes II (145–116 BCE) took over, he reversed the policy of Ptolemy VI and seems to have instigated an immediate threat to the Jews (again, for political reasons), but this was withdrawn. Popular memory turned it into a miraculous deliverance; however, the actual situation was probably more prosaic: Ptolemy VIII married Cleopatra III, and his policy suddenly changed rather drastically. He appears to have advanced the cause of both Jews and Egyptians in a bid to curb the power of the Greeks, which may have begun some of the animosity so strongly expressed in the Roman period. He seems even to have given some Jews the privileges of citizenship as a part of this scheme. Cleopatra III continued this policy after the death of her husband, evidently relying heavily on two Jewish generals (which naturally roused the jealousy of other high officials and may have led to some future tradition of hostility).

The Seleucids

The Seleucid empire covered an enormous territory, at least in its early phase. Many Jewish communities lived under its rule—in Babylon, Asia Minor, and Syria. Mesopotamia was lost to the Arsacids about 251, and the Jewish community in Babylon developed under an Oriental dynasty. The Jewish communities under Seleucid rule are not often referred to, but we have some attestation of them in such major cities as

Antioch and Damascus. Most of our knowledge comes from the
Roman period, however (pp. 85-87).

It is the Jews in Judea that we know most about under Seleucid rule.
The Hellenization process which had been going on for over a century
culminated in what has been called the 'Hellenistic reform' in
Jerusalem. Shortly after Antiochus IV Epiphanes took the Seleucid
throne in 175 BCE, Jason instigated a coup against his brother, the high
priest Onias III. He offered Antiochus a large sum of money (possibly
an annual payment) to have the office given to him. He promised an
additional sum to be given the opportunity to set up a gymnasium and
establish an ephebate and a list of citizens. It seems that Jason had
obtained permission for Jerusalem to be made into a Greek city or *polis*.
A Greek foundation would have a gymnasium as an educational institu-
tion to train the youth (those on the ephebate list or the future citizens), and also as a social and cultural centre. In addition, the enrolled
citizens would have the privilege and responsibility of governing the
city, whether through a council of elders (*gerousia*) or an assembly or a
combination.

This episode in Jewish history has often been misunderstood. Although Jason usurped the priesthood, he continued the traditional
temple ritual and Jewish worship. The allegations that he breached
Jewish law or engaged in pagan worship have no foundation in the
sources. Indeed, since the financial and power base of the high priesthood lay in the temple, it would not have been in his interest to risk
losing the tithes or offerings of the people. The adoption of certain
Hellenistic institutions did not constitute a violation of Jewish law as
long as the religion was not affected. Jewish law was definitely broken
under Menelaus, who took away the high priesthood in his turn, but it
is also doubtful that he continued the 'Hellenistic reform'.

The important consideration for our purposes is that Greek language,
culture, and education were all available to Jews in Jerusalem at this
time. They were not necessarily available to all Jews, but to those of the
upper social strata, the ability to read and write Greek and even a
knowledge of Greek literature seem to have been common. There is no
reason why such a book as the Wisdom of Solomon could not have
been written in Jerusalem or perhaps even elsewhere in the Palestinian
area.

The Hasmoneans

The Maccabean revolt was a reaction to the suppression of Judaism.
About December 168 BCE, after a series of events which is still unclear,

the daily sacrifice was stopped in the temple and an 'abomination of desolation' was set up in the temple. A new cult was substituted under the orders of Antiochus IV, and the practice of Judaism was outlawed, at least in Judea. Resistance immediately developed to this act, a resistance eventually dominated by the Maccabean brothers (though it is not certain that they actually began it). After three years, the temple was retaken from the Syrian garrison, it was ritually purified, and the sacrificial cult reinstated, probably in December 165. About a year later Antiochus withdrew the decree outlawing Judaism, and Jews were once again in a position to practice their religion. Many Jews were satisfied with the renewed status quo; only the Maccabees and a few followers continued to resist. After many years on the run, they eventually began to gain successes through diplomatic maneuvering. Judas was killed fighting, but Jonathan gained the high priesthood. After his death, it was passed to Simon, under whose rule the Hasmonean state can be said to have begun officially in 140 BCE.

It would be incorrect to call the Maccabean revolt a revolt against Hellenization, if one means that the Maccabees aimed to reverse the process of cultural Hellenization which had been going on for close to two centuries. It was, rather, a revolt against religious suppression. Most Jews were content with things as they were as soon as freedom to practice their religion was restored. When the Maccabeans took control, there does not seem to have been any change in this area. Rather the Hasmonean court was a typically Hellenistic one. Even the main records of the revolt were given in the Greek language. True, 1 Maccabees was originally written in Hebrew, but a Greek translation was soon made and seems to be the main version known. As for 2 Maccabees it is an epitome or cut-down version of Jason of Cyrene's account written originally in Greek. The process of Hellenization, far from being resisted by the Jews, continued on at a steady pace.

The Romans

After almost a century as a more-or-less independent state, Judea came under Roman conrol in 63 BCE. The fortunes of the Jews were initially closely tied to events in the Roman civil war. The Jews proved themselves useful to the Romans, assisting them in taking Egypt in 47 BCE. The Romans rewarded the two leaders, Hyrcanus and Antipas (the father of Herod), with Roman citizenship. It has been suggested that the animosity between the Greek and the Jewish community in Alexandria began at this time. The Greeks would have seen the Jews as traitors who sided with the enemies of the Ptolemaic dynasty.

The Parthian invasion and its threat to Rome helped bring Herod to
the throne as a Roman 'friendly king' or 'client king' in 40 BCE. His
many building projects and other aspects of his reign fitted well the
Hellenistic world of which Judea was a part. Even the refurbished temple was evidently a supreme example of Hellenistic architecture. Herod
died in 4 BCE; his son reigned until 6 CE. Except for the brief few years
under Agrippa I (41–44 CE), Judea was now a Roman province, under
Roman governors. Agrippa II, Agrippa I's son, had certain rights and
influence in Jerusalem after his father's death, even though he was not
king over Judea, until the beginning of the war with Rome in 66 CE.

The smoldering conflict between Greeks and Jews in Egypt grew
worse during the early decades of the first century. In 24–23 BCE the
Jews were made liable for the *laographia*, a type of poll tax which applied
to the native Egyptians but from which the Greeks were exempt. When
the Jews were subjected to it, it was not only a financial burden but also
a sign of lower status. Only the very few Jews who were citizens were
exempt. Not surprisingly some Jews began to try to find ways of gaining
the status of citizen. This was one of the reasons—if not necessarily the
only one—which led to the outbreak of riots against the Jewish community in 38 CE. The Roman governor Flaccus seems to have done
little to suppress the violence or protect the Jews. So in 39 or 40 Philo
was designated to lead a delegation to the Roman emperor Gaius, better
known as Caligula (37–41 CE).

It was while Philo was in Rome, awaiting an audience with the emperor, that a new threat to Jewish religion emerged in the year 40.
Caligula announced plans to set up a statue of himself in the Jerusalem
temple. The reasons why he made this decision are complex, though
recent study suggests it was not just caprice or megalomania on his part.
But whatever the reason, it presented a severe crisis for Jews. It conjured
up shades of Antiochus IV, the 'abomination of desolation' in the
temple, and the suppression of Judaism as a religion. The threat was
eventually withdrawn, apparently in large part because of the appeal of
Agrippa I to Caligula, and the desecration of the temple did not take
place. Even so, on only a handful of other occasions had Judaism been
so menaced in its history up to that time. And it left its mark in the
literature.

The difficulties of the Alexandrian community were partially resolved
by a decree of the emperor Claudius in 41. He instructed the Greeks to
leave the Jews alone, but he also told the Jews not to seek citizenship
and not to invite their fellow countrymen to come live in Alexandria.

Neither side can have been happy with this, but it seems to have stopped the overt conflicts for the time being. It was nearly a century later that the Jewish community in Alexandria was dealt a devastating blow. The Jews in Mesopotamia, Cyprus, and Egypt revolted against Roman rule in 115–17. As a result, the community in Alexandria was decimated and the magnificent synagogue destroyed.

Jewish communities were found in many other places. There were Jews in many cities in Syria and Asia Minor, as indicated by Josephus and also the New Testament book of Acts. They contributed a good deal of money to the Jerusalem temple. Jews had already migrated to Rome perhaps as early as the Hasmonean period. Many seem to have been taken captive after the Romans took Jerusalem in 63 BCE. As time went on, many of these or their descendants were freed, and the Jewish community began to grow. Most of them would not have been of very high status, but there were probably some educated individuals among them.

Date of Composition

Now that the possible contexts for the book have been discussed in the previous section, we can begin to ask where the Wisdom of Solomon might fit into this history. A variety of dates has been proposed, ranging from the third century BCE to the second century CE (see the survey in Larcher 1983–85: I, 141-46). The more extreme dates, such as a composition as late as 180 CE, have been almost universally rejected. A number of the early dates have depended on a supposed link with persecutions of the Jews during the time of Ptolemy IV Philopator (221–204 BCE), VI Philometor (180–145 BCE), VIII Physcon (145–116 BCE). These have two problems: (a) the Wisdom of Solomon gives no clear indications of persecutions as a part of its context; (b) as noted above (p. 83) the alleged persecutions under these kings are likely to be later Jewish propaganda as, e.g., in 3 Maccabees. The first real evidence of antipathy to the Jews on the part of the Greeks of Egypt seems no earlier than the reign of Cleopatra III (c. 140–100 BCE) who favored them (Tcherikover *et al.* 1957–64: I, 22-25). There are also stories that persecutions took place under her successors, Ptolemy IX Lathyros (116–107, 88–80 BCE) or Ptolemy X Alexander (107–88 BCE). In any case, the main friction seems to have developed after the Roman conquest of Egypt in which the Jews actively supported the Romans.

Perhaps the most conventional position in the recent past has been to date the book to the first century BCE, usually the period after the

Roman conquest of Egypt in 47 BCE. One of the most detailed arguments supporting this is given by Larcher (1983–85: I, 148-61), who thinks it was composed by one author in the period approximately 31–10 BCE. In addition to the question of persecutions, a number of arguments have been used in favor of the first century BCE:

1. The Septuagint translation of the book of Isaiah seems to be quoted in 2.12 (cf. Isa. 3.10) and 15.10 (cf. Isa. 44.20). Of course, the question of how early Isaiah was translated into Greek is not an easy one to answer; however, the translation is likely to have been complete by 100 BCE.

2. Some passages of the New Testament seem to be dependent on the Wisdom of Solomon at various points. This is a very subjective opinion. No New Testament passage is clearly a quotation from the Wisdom of Solomon, though some are fairly close. The two books could have been drawing on a common store of thought rather than having some sort of literary dependence (see further at pp. 28-29).

3. Wis. 3.9 appears to make use of 1 En. 5.7 but in its Greek version. If so, the Wisdom of Solomon is later than the translation of 1 Enoch into Greek. Again, though, it is not known when 1 Enoch or even this section of 1 Enoch was translated from its original Aramaic (now known from manuscripts found at Qumran).

More recently a strong argument has been made for dating the book about the time of Caligula, i.e., about 37–41 CE (Winston 1979: 20-25; Cheon). Some of the main points in defence of this position are as follows.

1. Wis. 6.1 refers to 'judges of the ends of the earth' ('judges' probably being used in the sense of 'rulers'). This has often been thought to suggest Roman rule. It fits Roman rule better than the Ptolemaic period.

2. Wis. 14.17 refers to remote rulers. This best fits the time of Augustus or later when Egypt was ruled from distant Rome.

3. Wis. 6.3 seems to refer to Augustus's conquest of Egypt, especially in the word *kratēsis* 'dominion'.

4. Wis. 5.16-23 gives an apocalyptic vision which best fits the time of Caligula and the threat to Judaism toward the end of his reign (p. 86).

5. The language of the book argues for the first part of the first century CE. Winston has found at least 35 words which are not attested as occurring in literature before the first century. It is true that usage is not always well reflected in existing literature; thus, words used for some time might not show up in literature until rather later, either because the words were not picked up by literary writers initially or because the writings which first used the words have not survived. If only a few words in the Wisdom of Solomon first occurred in first-century literature, this might be due to historical accident. However, when the number is no fewer than 35, it seems unlikely that this is only accidental.

6. The criticisms of idolatrous worship appear to reflect the situation under the Romans rather than under the Ptolemies. The Ptolemaic rulers had made explicit claim to being gods (*theoi*) and had their own cults even while alive. Assimilation of the Roman emperor to divine status developed only gradually in the early Empire. Thus, Wis. 14.26-30 seems to fit better with the early Roman empire than the previous period.

As noted above, the more extreme dates are generally rejected. There are general indications which might suit late Ptolemaic or early Roman rule. Much of the affirmation for Ptolemaic rule depends on the assumption that the Jews were being persecuted. There is little evidence of this before the Roman period. The references to idolatry seem better to fit Roman rule than Ptolemaic.

The arguments for the reign of Caligula are well presented, but some of the points just made would be consistent with any time in the early Empire. The strongest argument seems to be that of language, and this cannot be decisive because literary attestation depends on the accidents of preservation. That is, the linguistic arguments seem quite strong for the early Roman period generally, but it is difficult to be so precise as the reign of Caligula. Specific references to that ruler's reign are also unclear. The main event affecting the Jews was his plan to put his own statue into the Jerusalem temple (p. 86). This would have been very traumatic if it had occurred. At the same time, the persecutions reached a climax with riots in 38 CE and following. The Wisdom of Solomon does not seem to have any direct reference to Caligula's plan, as one might expect, nor are the references to the 'wicked' so specific as to suggest the period 38–41. The Wisdom of Solomon seems to be speaking generally and not out of the pain of a present acute reality, with blows falling continually on the Jewish community. Unless the author was exercising remarkable restraint or was well removed from the events affecting the Jews widely in the Roman empire, the reign of Caligula does not seem the best setting for the book.

Therefore, it seems to me that the best time is the reign of Augustus. Nevertheless, the reader should be aware that there are no conclusive means of dating the book, only a convergence of indicators, and that reputable scholars have proposed other dates. This is why it is important to keep in mind the broad picture of Jewish history and culture for this general period of time.

Place of Writing

There is no reason why a book like the Wisdom of Solomon could not have been written in a variety of places in the ancient Near East. The Hellenistic world encompassed the entire eastern part of the Mediterranean. It included Palestine as well as Asia Minor, Syria, and Egypt. We know of Jewish Hellenistic literature produced in Palestine, so it is theoretically possible that the the Wisdom of Solomon was written even in Jerusalem, the heart of Judaism itself. Nevertheless, scholars have been almost unanimous in arguing for Egypt. The reasons are the following:

1. Wis. 19.13-17 makes a point of the wickedness of Egypt: it is said to be worse than the legendary Sodom. There seems little reason to single out Egypt unless the writer is speaking from the heart from personal knowledge. That is, the sins of Egypt were so well known to his audience that the author felt compelled to speak out against them.

2. Wis. 17.16 has allusions to *anachōrēsis* 'withdrawal', a sort of 'strike' by peasants who fled to the desert or elsewhere to hide when the tax burden became too great.

3. Although hatred for Egypt is expressed, it is not as sharp as in *Sib. Or.* 5 which arose in the early second century CE.

The strongest argument is the first one, but it must also be said that the exodus is a strong tradition throughout Judaism. One could use it as a cornerstone of a theological treatise without also living in Egypt. Thus, the centrality of Egypt to the book does not prove Egyptian provenance. On the other hand, if it was not composed in Alexandria, it is difficult to point to another specific place in the Hellenistic world. That still seems the most probable place, even if it is not certain.

Audience

The audience and dating of the book are often intimately connected. The dating is deduced from the assumed readership, and the assumed readership often depends heavily on when a scholar thinks the book was written. The dangers of circular reading should be readily apparent!

The Wisdom of Solomon addresses a variety of issues, some of which imply a particular audience. There is nothing to prevent the writer having educated Greco–Romans in mind. A number of Jewish writings seem to be written to such an audience, often with an apologetic function. A good example of Jewish apologetic is Josephus's *Antiquities* or his *Against Apion* in which he seeks to display Judaism in a good light for non-Jews. Similarly, Pseudo-Phocylides seeks to use a Greek literary form to convey its message to non-Jews; indeed, it is so successful that there is still occasional dispute as to whether it is a Jewish work or not. The Jewish *Sibylline Oracles* also have a pagan audience in mind, but their function is quite different. They seek to *deceive* the readers into thinking that genuine Sibylline Oracles had predicted the things contained in them. To any readers—whether Jew or non-Jew—the vindication of the Jews would appear to be prophesied by a non-Jewish oracle.

There is a good deal in the Wisdom of Solomon which could have a Gentile audience potentially in mind. For example, the book begins with an address to the 'judges of the earth' (1.1). Wisdom 6–9 also addresses the rulers of the earth. Is this a genuine attempt to get a message across to kings and governors? Much of the content of chs. 1–5, with its emphasis on morality and piety, could be relevant to an audience of religious non-Jews. Also, as noted at p. 66, here and there is a section which could be seen as an apology directed at non-Jews. But in the book is also a good deal of Jewish material which was unlikely to have much meaning for the non-Jew. Either the writer was extremely naive about how to reach the audience, or at no time had an exclusively—or even primarily—Gentile audience in mind. It has been noted that Wisdom 7–10 might be suitable for a general audience with a sort of 'natural theology', but from ch. 11 the writer focuses specifically on Jewish tradition, and a non-Jew would be unlikely to understand what was being argued (Schwenk-Bressler 1993: 341-44).

In Wisdom 1–5 the righteous are clearly defined as those who follow the Jewish law. The Israelite God is presupposed in much of the book; no Greek or Roman writing would refer to the gods in this way. More important are the many references to passages in the Septuagint and to Jewish tradition in general. This stands out particularly in 10–19 where the biblical history between Adam and the exodus is rehearsed, the plagues are enumerated, and idolatry is attacked at length. The figure of wisdom herself is best paralleled in Jewish tradition, even though she has some traits in common with Greek and Near Eastern goddess figures (especially Isis).

J.M. Reese has argued that the writer has in mind the Jewish youth of Alexandria. These were likely to have been attracted by the literature of Isis worship (1970: 40). Therefore, the Wisdom of Solomon uses Isis language, figures, and forms to address this audience with the aim of weaning it off the Isis cult and wooing it back to 'true' Judaism. His arguments can be summarized under two points (1970: 36-50): (a) there are many epithets and characteristics of Isis which are also applied to wisdom in the Wisdom of Solomon; (b) Wis. 6.22–10.21 has the same structure as an Isis aretalogy, i.e., a hymn or poem in praise of Isis. The Isis aretalogy has four parts which correspond to this section of the Wisdom of Solomon, according to Reese. Part 1 on the nature and origin of Isis is similar to Wis. 7.22–8.1 on wisdom; part 2 on Isis' powers is parallel to Wis. 8.2-18 which lists the various characteristics of wisdom; part 3 on Isis' benefits corresponds well with Wisdom 10 which lists wisdom's benefits. The Isis aretalogy ends with an invocation of the deity. The Wisdom of Solomon does not have this but does have a prayer asking for wisdom (ch. 9). The writer has also added his own introduction to this section in the form of an autobiographical narrative in 7.1-22.

Reese's position has been opposed by J.S. Kloppenborg (1982: 60-61). He finds problems with Reese's list of attributes, arguing that in a number of cases the comparison does not stand up to scrutiny; however, he accepts that a more careful survey of the Isis material would probably yield an extensive set of parallels. The problem is that these were part of the general parcel of divine attributes which could be used for a variety of deities. As for the alleged aretalogical form of Wis. 6–10, Kloppenborg is very skeptical. Although there are parallels, the Isis aretalogy itself is based on the general form of the Greek hymn, so the Wisdom of Solomon could be imitating merely the general hymnic form. More specifically, some of the parallels put forward by Reese are not in fact convincing. Thus, despite the ingenuity of Reese's argument, it is difficult to follow him in seeing a specific opposition to the Isis cult. One suspects that the author of the Wisdom of Solomon would have been more explicit in his attack on the Isis cult if this was the main threat perceived by him.

Schwenk-Bressler (1993: 267-69, 274-75, 343-47) has noted that some passages of the Wisdom of Solomon present Judaism in the form of a mystery religion. For example, the Passover is presented as a secret offering; and the passage through the Red Sea, as a new birth, corresponding to the concept of a new birth in the mysteries. Judaism comes across as a very old mystery, in contrast to the pagan mystery cults which are 'modern'. As already noted, some of the vocabulary of the book is that of the mystery religions (pp. 35-36 above). Thus, it may be that rather than the Isis cult in particular, the mystery cults in general are in the mind of the writer.

The most likely audience is the educated Jewish youth of Alexandria who found the surrounding Hellenistic culture attractive, including the various cults, and might be tempted to abandon Judaism altogether. That such might happen can be exemplified from even the very family of Philo. According to Josephus, Philo's nephew Tiberius Alexander (to whom Philo addressed one of his tractates) had abandoned his ancestral religion (*Ant.* 20.5.2 §100). Except for the matter of religion, there was little to prevent educated young Jewish men from partaking of the delights of Greek culture glittering all round them, as Philo himself seems to have done at one time in his life.

But was it just a case of the attractions, or did the Jews experience an equal danger from oppression? In other words, were they both attracted away from Judaism by the lure of Greek society and equally driven away from Judaism by the lower status, discrimination, and perhaps even persecution against Jews? Both are possibilities, depending on when the book was written, though it is interesting that persecution from the larger society against a small community tends to bring the latter together. In the case of oppression, the Wisdom of Solomon could have served as a form of encouragement. As Kloppenborg notes (1982: 64),

> Pseudo-Solomon aims at providing Jews with a means of self-definition over against paganism through identification with the reputation, wisdom, and success of Solomon, *sophos par excellence* and esteemed teacher of pagan kings.

It is probable that the Wisdom of Solomon had several aims. One of the main ones is likely to have been encouragement of the Jewish community, especially the young men, in the face of dangers from the larger Greco–Roman society, including the attractions of the mystery and other religious cults. Another would have been to teach members of the community the importance of seeking and gaining wisdom. The moral aim of the book is also clear. It cannot be ruled out that the author also wanted to reach a Greco–Roman readership, but this would have been a secondary aim at best.

Conclusions

The potential context for the Wisdom of Solomon covers a large area and a large span of time. Recent study has generally abandoned the idea that parts of it were originally composed in a Semitic language, and we can safely take it as an original composition in Greek. Therefore, a writing such as this could have arisen pretty much any time after the coming of Alexander, and it could have come from anywhere in the Hellenistic world. As so often with Jewish literature, there are no clear statements about time or place of writing, and one must be careful not to overinterpret the evidence. But there are indications in the book itself which limit the possibilities.

The Wisdom of Solomon is unlikely to have been written early in the Ptolemaic period. There is some evidence of persecution even if the references are not all that specific. This probably came later rather than earlier. More decisive is linguistic usage. Although dating by language is not a precise science, the large amount of Greek material preserved from this period helps to narrow the field. The large number of words attested only in late writings suggests the book is unlikely to have been composed earlier than the Roman period. It has been suggested that the vocabulary argues for the first century CE, but it seems that this dating implies a precision rather greater than is actually possible—one can only say that it was probably the early Roman empire. Against this is the lack of any clear reference to Caligula's attempt to place his statue in the temple. Thus, it seems to me that those who put the book in the reign of Augustus presently hold the balance of the argument. Nevertheless, dating is difficult and it would hardly do to be dogmatic other than to suggest that the early Roman period is the best context from data currently available.

Although the audience may possibly have included Greco–Roman readers, the most direct target of the author is likely to have been the Jewish community. It probably included the aim of encouraging the community in the face of difficulties and perhaps even the threat that the surrounding Hellenistic culture might attract some away from their religion, especially young people of the community. This last point is suggested by the number of subtle references to the mystery and related cults in the environment of the community. The problem with being more precise is that dating and audience are often closely associated. It would certainly make the one easier to deal with if the other could be established beyond reasonable doubt.

Further Reading

For more information on the history of the Jews, especially in Palestine, during the Greek and early Roman periods, see Grabbe (1992). Some of the same ground is covered in less detailed but simpler form in Grabbe (1996).

For a detailed discussion of Hellenization and its impact on the Jews, including an inter-action with some of the main discussions and a listing of the most important secondary studies, see Grabbe (1992: ch. 3; 1995a).

For specific studies on Jewish communities outside Palestine, see Applebaum (1979); Leon (1960); Rutgers (1995); Tcherikover *et al.* (1957–64); Trebilco (1991).

On the dating, see Cheon (forthcoming); Gilbert (1986: 91-93); Winston (1979: 20-25).

On the audience, see Collins (1977–78: 121-42); Kloppenborg (1982: 57-84); Reese (1970).

Bibliography

Albright, William F.
    1919–20   'The Goddess of Life and Wisdom', *AJSL* 36: 258-94.

Applebaum, S.
    1979   *Jews and Greeks in Ancient Cyrene* (SJLA, 28; Leiden: Brill).

Barr, James
    1961   *The Semantics of Biblical Language* (Oxford: Clarendon Press).
    1966   *Old and New in Interpretation* (London: SCM Press).

Brunner, Hellmut
    1958   'Gerechtigkeit als Fundament des Thrones', *VT* 8: 426-28.

Cheon, Samuel
    forthcoming   *Exodus in the Wisdom of Solomon: A Study in Biblical Interpretation* (JSPSup, 23; Sheffield: Sheffield Academic Press).

Charlesworth, James H.
    1980   'The Portrayal of the Righteous as an Angel', in J.J. Collins and G.W.E. Nickelsburg (eds.), *Ideal Figures in Ancient Judaism: Profiles and Paradigms* (SBLSCS, 12; Atlanta: Scholars Press): 135-51.

Childs, Brevard S.
    1970   *Biblical Theology in Crisis* (Philadelphia: Westminster).

Clarke, E.G.
    1973   *The Wisdom of Solomon* (Cambridge Bible Commentary on the New English Bible; Cambridge University Press).

Collins, John J.
    1974   'Apocalyptic Eschatology as the Transcendence of Death', *CBQ* 36: 21-43.
    1977–78   'Cosmos and Salvation: Jewish Wisdom and Apocalyptic in the Hellenistic Age', *HR* 17: 121-42.
    1984   *The Apocalyptic Imagination: An Introduction to the Jewish Matrix of Christianity* (New York: Crossroad).
    1986   *Between Athens and Jerusalem: Jewish Identity in the Hellenistic Diaspora* (New York: Crossroad).

Dalbert, Peter
    1954   *Die Theologie der hellenistisch-jüdischen Missionsliteratur unter Ausschluss von Philo und Josephus* (Theologische Forschung, 4; Hamburg–Volksdorf: Herbert Reich).

Dever, William G.
    1984   'Asherah, Consort of Yahweh? New Evidence from Kuntillet 'Ajrûd', *BASOR* 255: 21-37.

Dupont-Sommer, A.
    1949   'De l'immortalité astrale dans la "Sagesse de Salomon" (III 7)', *Revue des Etudes Grecques* 62: 80-87.

Düring, Ingemar
    1961   *Aristotle's Protrepticus: An Attempt at Reconstruction* (Studia Graeca et Latina
            Gothoburgensia, 12; Göteborg: Acta Universitatis Gothoburgensis).
Emerton, John A., and David J. Lane (eds.)
    1979   *Wisdom of Solomon* (Old Testament in Syriac, 2.5; Leiden: Brill).
Fischel, Henry A.
    1973   'The Uses of Sorites (*Climax, Gradatio*) in the Tannaitic Period', *HUCA*
            54: 119-51.
Focke, Friedrich
    1913   *Die Entstehung der Weisheit Salomos: Ein Beitrag zur Geschichte des jüdischen
            Hellenismus* (FRLANT, 22; Göttingen: Vandenhoeck & Ruprecht).
Georgi, Dieter
    1980   *Weisheit Salomos* (JSHRZ, 3.4; Gütersloh: Mohn): 391-478.
Gilbert, M., SJ
    1970   'La structure de la prière de Salomon (Sg 9)', *Bib* 51: 301-31.
    1973   *La critique des dieux dans le Livre de la Sagesse (Sg 13–15)* (AnBib, 53;
            Rome: Biblical Institute).
    1984   'Wisdom of Solomon', in M.E. Stone (ed.), *Jewish Writings of the Second
            Temple Period: Apocrypha, Pseudepigrapha, Qumran Sectarian Writings, Philo,
            Josephus* (CRINT, 2.2; Assen: Van Gorcum; Minneapolis: Fortress Press):
            301-13.
    1986   'Sagesse de Salomon (ou Livre de la Sagesse)', in J. Briend and E.
            Cothenet (eds.), *Supplément au Dictionnaire de la Bible* (Paris: Letouzey &
            Ané): XI, 58-119.
Goldstein, Jonathan
    1984   'The Origins of the Doctrine of Creation Ex Nihilo', *JJS* 35: 127-35.
    1987   'Creation Ex Nihilo: Recantations and Restatements', *JJS* 38: 187-94.
Goodenough, Edwin R.
    1962   *An Introduction to Philo Judaeus* (Oxford: Clarendon, rev. edn).
Grabbe, Lester L.
    1979   'The Jannes/Jambres Tradition in Targum Pseudo-Jonathan and its
            Date', *JBL* 98: 393-401.
    1988   *Etymology in Early Jewish Interpretation: The Hebrew Names in Philo* (BJS,
            115; Atlanta: Scholars Press).
    1991   'Philo and Aggada: A Response to B.J. Bamberger', in D.T. Runia *et al.*
            (eds.), *Heirs of the Septuagint: Philo, Hellenistic Judaism and Early
            Christianity: Festschrift for Earle Hilgert* (Atlanta: Scholars Press) = Studia
            Philonica Annual 3: 153-66.
    1992   *Judaism from Cyrus to Hadrian. I. Persian and Greek Periods. II. Roman Period*
            (Minneapolis: Fortress Press; one-volume edition, London: SCM Press,
            1994).
    1995a   'Hellenistic Judaism', in J. Neusner (ed.), *Judaism in Late Antiquity. II.
            Historical Syntheses* (Handbuch der Orientalistik: Erste Abteilung, Der
            Nahe und Mittlere Osten, Bd. 17; Leiden: Brill): 53-83.
    1995b   *Priests, Prophets, Diviners, Sages: A Socio-historical Study of Religious
            Specialists in Ancient Israel* (Valley Forge, PA: Trinity Press International).
    1996   *An Introduction to First Century Judaism: Religion and Politics 539 BCE to 135
            CE* (Edinburgh: T. & T. Clark).

Grant, Robert M.
    1966   'The Book of Wisdom at Alexandria: Reflections on the History of the
               Canon and Theology', in F.L. Cross (ed.), *Studia Patristica VII: Papers Pre-
               sented to the Fourth International Conference on Patristic Studies Held at Christ
               Church, Oxford, 1963* (TU, 92; Berlin: Akademie-Verlag): I, 462-72.

Grimm, C.L.W.
    1837   *Commentar über das Buch der Weisheit* (Leipzig: Hochhausen und Fournes).
    1860   *Das Buch der Weisheit erklärt* (Kurzgefasstes exegetisches Handbuch zu den
               Apokryphen des Alten Testaments, part 6; Leipzig: Hirzel).

Heinemann, Isaak
    1932   *Philons griechische und jüdische Bildung* (reprinted with additional notes,
               Hildesheim: Olms, 1962).
    1948   'Synkrisis oder äussere Analogie in der "Weisheit Salomos" ', *TZ* 4: 241-
               51.

Hengel, Martin
    1974   *Judaism and Hellenism* (2 vols.; London: SCM Press; Philadelphia: Fortress
               Press).

Hock, Ronald F., and Edward N. O'Neil (eds.)
    1986   *The Chreia in Ancient Rhetoric. I. The Progymnasmata* (Texts and Trans-
               lations 27; Graeco-Roman Religion Series, 9; Atlanta: Scholars Press).

Holladay, Carl R.
    1983   *Fragments from Hellenistic Jewish Authors. I. Historians* (SBLTT, 20; Pseud-
               epigrapha Series, 10; Atlanta: Scholars Press).
    1989   *Fragments from Hellenistic Jewish Authors. II. Poets: The Epic Poets Theodotus
               and Philo and Ezekiel the Tragedian* (SBLTT, 30; Pseudepigrapha Series,
               12; Atlanta: Scholars Press).
    1995   *Fragments from Hellenistic Jewish Authors. III. Aristobulus* (SBLTT, 39;
               Pseudepigrapha Series, 13; Atlanta: Scholars Press).

Holmes, Samuel
    1913   'The Wisdom of Solomon', in R.H. Charles (ed.), *The Apocrypha and
               Pseudepigrapha of the Old Testament in English* (Oxford: Clarendon), I,
               518-68.

Kayatz, Christa
    1966   *Studien zu Proverbien 1–9: Eine form- und motivgeschichtliche Untersuchung
               unter Einbeziehung ägyptischen Vergleichsmaterials* (WMANT, 22;
               Neukirchen–Vluyn: Neukirchen Verlag).

Kloppenborg, John S.
    1982   'Isis and Sophia in the Book of Wisdom', *HTR* 75: 57-84.

Knibb, M.A.
    1978   *The Ethiopic Book of Enoch* (vols. I–II; Oxford: Clarendon).

Kolarcik, Michael
    1991   *The Ambiguity of Death in the Book of Wisdom 1–6: A Study of Literary
               Structure and Interpretation* (AnBib, 127; Rome: Pontifical Biblical
               Institute).

Lang, Bernhard
    1986   *Wisdom and the Book of Proverbs: An Israelite Goddess Redefined* (New
               York: Pilgrim Press).

Larcher, C., OP
    1969   *Etudes sur le Livre de la Sagesse* (EBib; Paris: Gabalda).
    1983–85 *Le Livre de la Sagesse ou la Sagesse de Salomon* (3 vols.; EBib, nouvelle série 1; Paris: Gabalda).

Lattimore, Richard
    1962   *Themes in Greek and Latin Epitaphs* (Urbana, IL: University of Illinois).

Leon, H.J.
    1960   *The Jews of Ancient Rome* (Morris Loeb Series; Philadelphia: Jewish Publication Society of America).

Lichtheim, Miriam
    1992   *Maat in Egyptian Autobiographies and Related Studies* (OBO, 120; Freiburg [Schweiz]: Universitätsverlag).

Lohse, E.
    1971   'Solomon', *TDNT* (ed. G. Kittel and G. Friedrich; Grand Rapids, MI: Eerdmans): VII, 459-65.

Long, A.A.
    1974   *Hellenistic Philosophy: Stoics, Epicureans, Sceptics* (London: Duckworth; New York: Scribner).

Mack, Burton L.
    1973   *Logos und Sophia: Untersuchungen zur Weisheitstheologie im hellenistischen Judentum* (SUNT, 10; Göttingen: Vandenhoeck & Ruprecht).
    1985   *Wisdom and the Hebrew Epic: Ben Sira's Hymn in Praise of the Fathers* (Chicago Studies in the History of Judaism; Chicago/London: University of Chicago).

Maier, Christl
    1995   *Die 'fremde Frau' in Proverbien 1–9: Eine exegetische und sozialgeschichtliche Studie* (OBO, 114; Freiburg [Schweiz]: Universitätsverlag; Göttingen: Vandenhoeck and Ruprecht).

Marcus, Ralph
    1950–51 'On Biblical Hypostases of Wisdom', *HUCA* 23: 157-71.

Mendels, Doron
    1987   *The Land of Israel as a Political Concept in Hasmonean Literature* (Texte und Studien zum Antiken Judentum, 15; Tübingen: Mohr [Paul Siebeck]).

Nickelsburg, G.W.E.
    1972   *Resurrection, Immortality, and Eternal Life in Intertestamental Judaism* (Harvard Theological Studies, 26; Cambridge, MA: Harvard).
    1981   *Jewish Literature between the Bible and the Mishnah* (Philadelphia: Fortress Press).

Pépin, J.
    1976   *Mythe et allégorie* (2nd edn; Paris: Etudes Augustiniennes).

Pfeiffer, Robert H.
    1949   *History of New Testament Times, with an Introduction to the Apocrypha* (New York: Harper).

Porten, B., and A. Yardeni (eds.)
    1993   *Textbook of Aramaic Documents from Ancient Egypt: 3 Literature, Accounts, Lists* (Hebrew University, Department of the History of the Jewish People, Texts and Studies for Students; Jerusalem: Hebrew University).

Porton, Gary G.
    1981   'Defining Midrash', in J. Neusner (ed.), *The Study of Ancient Judaism I:
                Mishnah, Midrash, Siddur* (New York: Ktav): 55-92 (revised from
                'Midrash: Palestinian Jews and the Hebrew Bible in the Greco–Roman
                Period', ANRW [Berlin/New York: de Gruyter, 1979]: II.19.2.103-38).
    1992   'Midrash', in D.N. Freedman *et al.* (eds.), *Anchor Bible Dictionary* (6 vols.;
                New York: Doubleday, 1992): IV, 818-22.

Reese, James M.
    1965   'Plan and Structure in the Book of Wisdom', *CBQ* 27: 391-99.
    1970   *Hellenistic Influence on the Book of Wisdom and Its Consequences* (AnBib, 41;
                Rome: Pontifical Biblical Institute).

Reider, J.
    1957   *The Book of Wisdom* (Jewish Apocryphal Literature; New York: Dropsie
                College).

Ringgren, Helmer
    1947   *Word and Wisdom: Studies in the Hypostatization of Divine Qualities and
                Functions in the Ancient Near East* (Lund: Ohlsson).

Rooden, Peter T. van
    1986   'Die antike Elementarlehre und der Aufbau von Sapientia Salomonis
                11–19', in J.W. van Henten *et al.* (eds.), *Tradition and Re-interpretation in
                Jewish and Early Christian Literature: Essays in Honour of Jürgen C.H. Lebram*
                (Studia Post-Biblica, 36; Leiden: Brill): 81-96.

Rutgers, Leonard Victor
    1995   *The Jews in Late Ancient Rome: Evidence of Cultural Interaction in the Roman
                Diaspora* (Religions in the Graeco–Roman World; Leiden: Brill).

Sanders, J.A.
    1967   *The Dead Sea Psalms Scroll* (Ithaca, NY: Cornell University).

Sandmel, Samuel
    1979   *Philo of Alexandria: An Introduction* (Oxford/New York: Oxford
                University Press).

Schaberg, Jane
    1982   'Major Midrashic Traditions in Wisdom 1,1–6,25', *JSJ* 8: 75-101.

Schürer, E.
    1973–86   'The Wisdom of Solomon', in G. Vermes, F. Millar and M. Goodman
                (eds.), *The History of the Jewish People in the Age of Jesus Christ (175 bc–ac.
                135)* (Edinburgh: T. & T. Clark, rev. edn), III, 568-79.

Schwenk-Bressler, Udo
    1993   *Sapientia Salomonis als ein Beispiel frühjüdischer Textauslegung: Die Auslegung
                des Buches Genesis, Exodus 1–15 und Teilen der Wüstentradition in Sap
                10–19* (Beiträge zur Erforschung des Alten Testaments und des antiken
                Judentums, 32; Frankfurt am Main: Lang).

Skehan, Patrick W.
    1945   'Text and Structure of the Book of Wisdom', Traditio 3: 1-12.
    1971   *Studies in Israelite Poetry and Wisdom* (CBQMS, 1; Washington, DC:
                Catholic Biblical Association).

Sowers, Stanley Kent
    1981   *The Diatribe and Paul's Letter to the Romans* (SBLDS, 57; Atlanta: Scholars
                Press).

Sparks, H. (ed.)
  1984   *Old Testament Apocrypha* (Oxford: Clarendon).
Stein, Edmund
  1934   'Ein jüdisch–hellenistischer Midrasch über den Auszug aus Ägypten',
             MGWJ 78: 558-75.
  1936   *'Sefer Ḥokmat Šělōmō', Ha-Sěfārîm ha-Ḥîṣônîm* (ed. Abraham Kehana;
             Tel-Aviv, 1936; reprinted Jerusalem: Makor, 1978): II, 363-414.
Suggs, M. Jack
  1957   'Wisdom of Solomon 2_{10-5}: A Homily Based on the Fourth Servant
             Song', *JBL* 76: 26-33.
Tcherikover, V.A., A. Fuks, and M. Stern
  1957–64   *Corpus Papyrorum Judaicarum* (3 vols.; Cambridge, MA: Harvard; Jeru-
             salem: Magnes).
Thiele, W. (ed.)
  1977–86   *Sapientia Salomonis* (Vetus Latina; Freiberg: Herder).
Trebilco, Paul R.
  1991   *Jewish Communities in Asia Minor* (SNTSMS, 69; Cambridge: Cambridge
             University Press).
Whybray, R.N.
  1965   *Wisdom in Proverbs: The Concepts of Wisdom in Proverbs 1–9* (Studies in
             Biblical Theology; London: SCM Press; Naperville, IL: Allenson).
  1994   *Proverbs* (NCB; London: Marshall Morgan and Scott; Grand Rapids, MI:
             Eerdmans).
Winston, David
  1971–72   'The Book of Wisdom's Theory of Cosmogony', *HR* 11: 185-202.
  1979   *The Wisdom of Solomon: A New Translation with Introduction and
             Commentary* (AB, 43; Garden City, NJ: Doubleday).
  1984   'Philo's Ethical Theory', *Aufstieg und Niedergang der römischen Welt: II
             Principat* (Berlin/New York: de Gruyter): 21.1.372-416.
  1986   'Creation Ex Nihilo Revisited: A Reply to Jonathan Goldstein', *JJS* 37:
             88-91.
  1992   'Solomon, Wisdom of', in D.N. Freedman *et al.* (eds.), *Anchor Bible
             Dictionary* (6 vols.; New York: Doubleday), VI, 120-27.
Wright, A.G.
  1965   'The Structure of Wisdom 11–19', *CBQ* 27: 28-34.
  1967a   'The Structure of the Book of Wisdom', *Bib* 48: 165-84.
  1967b   'Numerical Patterns in the Book of Wisdom', *CBQ* 29: 524-38.
Zevit, Ziony
  1984   'The Khirbet el-Qom Inscription Mentioning a Goddess', *BASOR* 255:
             39-47
Ziegler, J.
  1980   *Sapientia Salomonis* (2nd edn; Septuaginta, Vetus Testamentum Graecum
             12/1; Göttingen: Vandenhoeck & Ruprecht).
Zimmerman, F.
  1966–67   'The Book of Wisdom: Its Language and Character', *JQR* 57: 1-27, 101-
             35.

INDEXES

INDEX OF REFERENCES

BIBLE

PSEUDEPIGRAPHA

INDEX OF AUTHORS